kosher by design

Kids in the Kitchen

by SUSIE FISHBEIN

Photographs by John Uher

Food Styling by Melanie Dubberley

Recipe Tester and Editor by Paula Shoyer

Graphic Design by Tzini Fruchthandler

Art Direction by Eli Kroen

Published by

Mesorah Publications, ltd

Published by ARTSCROLL / SHAAR PRESS
4401 Second Avenue / Brooklyn, NY 11232 / (718) 921-9000
www.artscroll.com • www.kosherbydesign.com

Distributed in Israel by SIFRIATI / A. GITLER
6 Hayarkon Street / Bnei Brak 51127 / Israel

Distributed in Europe by LEHMANNS
Unit E, Viking Business Park, Rolling Mill Road
Jarrow, Tyne and Wear, NE32 3DP / England

Distributed in Australia and New Zealand by GOLDS WORLD OF JUDAICA
3-13 William Street / Balaclava, Melbourne 3183, Victoria / Australia

Distributed in South Africa by KOLLEL BOOKSHOP
Shop 8A Norwood Hypermarket / Norwood 2196 / Johannesburg, South Africa

ISBN: 1-57819-071-1

Printed in the USA by Noble Book Press

Whether in the kitchen or anywhere,
this book is dedicated to my favorite kids

Kate, Danielle, Jodi, Eli

and of course, to my biggest kid, Kalman

Thank you to my fabulous team of kid testers. I love how seriously
you took your job and I know we all loved tasting your results.

Mollie Adolf, Alex Brizel, Mindie Erreich, Danielle Fishbein, Kate Fishbein,

Jodi Fishbein, Arianna Gorkowitz, Hannah Gurmankin, Danna Homa,

Noa Hubsher, Zellie Hubsher, Julia Krevat, Sarah Krevat, Josh Krieger,

Sophie Lewittes, Jonathan Murray, Julie Murray, Talya Presser, Zahava Presser,

Julianna Stadtmauer, Steven Wengrofsky, Ari Zucker, and Rachel Zucker

Dear Grown-ups,

Welcome your kids to the kitchen!

Maybe it's the one-on-one time with a parent or grandparent. Maybe it's the getting messy part, or maybe it's the gratification of enjoying and sharing the fruits of their labor. What is undeniable is that kids love to cook, all kids, all ages, both genders. This book is about getting kids into the kitchen.

So whether you are the parent who loves to cook and wants to pass on that positive experience, or you are the parent who feels inept or uncomfortable in the kitchen and, doesn't want to pass that on, here's your chance to start again from a kid's perspective.

The recipes in the book are for real food, nothing silly like gummy worms crawling out of cookie crumbs. They are for foods that kids universally love as well as some starter ideas for simple meals. The concept is to challenge kids and to inspire them to want to cook more.

As kids grow to be comfortable in the kitchen, they will become more independent and gain a better awareness of what they are eating. The best way to get kids to try a new food is to have them prepare it. Nutritionally speaking, looking at a food pyramid is meaningless to a child. An invaluable lesson can be learned when children see foods in their raw form and learn how to use the ingredients to turn out fresh, fabulous dishes. When children see just how much sugar there is in "a cup of sugar," they are given a new perspective for healthful eating.

Be on hand to supervise but try not to intervene. Get involved where there is a safety issue like using sharp knives, setting up an appliance, or moving a heavy pot, but resist the urge to jump in throughout the process. Take the time to show your kids around the kitchen. Demonstrate the safe way to use each appliance and utensil. Let them know which ones may be off-limits based on their ages.

In the beginning, you and your kids may not be creating gourmet meals but you will be creating memories and skills that will last a lifetime.

Enjoy,
Susie

Hey Kids,

Welcome to the kitchen!

Cooking is a fun way to spend time with your friends and family, and sharing what you make with them is even more fun! The book is filled with recipes you love and ingredients you'll find appealing. These are recipes for you to learn as a kid but I know you will use them even after you are a grown-up. Many of these dishes are things I made with my mom when I was younger, and I still make them today. Each recipe is coded using a chef's hat system, that features one, two, or three hats to show the level of difficulty.  *One hat indicates the easiest level, using the fewest cooking skills — anyone can begin here. Two-hat recipes require some cutting skills and standard equipment. Three-hat recipes are for those of you already comfortable in the kitchen.*

One of my favorite parts of cooking is that you are free to experiment. Try the recipes as written but then go back and add your special flair, like different spices or toppings for a new taste sensation. Once you become comfortable in the kitchen, there will be no stopping you. You will never need to wait again for someone to prepare a snack or a meal for you. Hey, you may even grow up and write your own cookbook!

Two tips to rule your kitchen:

1 *The French term, "mise en place" should rule your kitchen. It means "everything in its place." Read through a recipe before you start cooking. Make sure you understand what you will be doing. An equipment list and ingredient list come with each recipe. Pre-measure and set out all of the tools you will need. If you have ever watched a cooking show, you will see that this is how the pros do it. This will keep you organized and prevent you from making errors halfway though a recipe. Even if it means washing out a few extra bowls that held the ingredients, it is worth it. It will also give your oven time to pre-heat, a very important step in successful cooking.*

2 *Clean up as you go. Keep a bowl on the counter to catch vegetable peelings, egg shells, wrappers, etc. This will avoid dripping as you make your way over to the garbage. It is neater and more efficient. After you use each piece of equipment, quickly wash and dry it and put it away. It is much easier to do this than to wait until the end, and it keeps the mess from getting out of control. Leaving your kitchen clean is key if you want to be invited back into it to cook!*

Enjoy,
Susie

Table of Contents

Safety Rules

Getting ready:

- Have an adult nearby to help.
- Wash your hands with warm water and soap before beginning.
- Tie back loose hair, avoid loose clothing, and take off jewelry.

The cutting edge:

- Always use a sharp knife. Choose one that feels comfortable in your hand.
- Remember to keep your fingers curled under so that you don't nick them while you are chopping or cutting.
- Always keep your knife on your cutting board, never on the edge of a counter where it may fall.
- Never leave a sharp knife in a sink loaded with dishes. You might not see it under other things or through soap bubbles and you might cut yourself.

Protect your mitts:

- Use oven mitts every time you take something out of the oven or lift a pot off the stove. Never use a wet towel to take something out of the oven — the wetness conducts the heat right to your hands. Ouch!
- Turn handles in when pots are on the stove so that you don't knock them over.
- Be careful of escaping steam when lifting the lid of a pot.

Stay out of the water:

- Never lift a heavy pot, especially one filled with boiling liquids. Spills can cause serious burns! Have an adult help you.
- Never use electrical appliances near the sink or other water sources. If your appliance falls into the sink, don't reach for it. Call an adult for help.
- Always unplug appliances before cleaning them.

How to Keep Your Kitchen Kosher

Be a Kosher label detective!

- Always look carefully at the labels on foods or ingredients you buy. It should have a reliable kosher symbol, which tells you that the food has been prepared under the supervision of rabbis who know all the laws of kashrut. Watch out! An R with an O around it is not a kosher symbol!

Meat and dairy never mix!

- Always keep meat foods (like hotdogs, beefburgers and chicken) and their utensils away from dairy foods (like ice cream, cheese and butter) and utensils.
- Foods that are neither meat nor dairy are called parve (like fish, eggs, vegetables, fruits, and flour). Parve utensils should be used only with parve foods.
- Whoops! If you think you made a mistake, don't be afraid to tell a grown-up about it. Let's say you used a meat pot for a dairy recipe. Your grown-up will be really glad you caught the mistake and will call a rabbi to ask what to do.

Yuk! Creepy crawly things don't belong in kosher food!

- Fresh fruits and vegetables must be checked by an adult to make sure there are no bugs or worms in them. On some kinds of produce, such as lettuce, they're really hard to see. Holding it up to the light will help you spot them.

Don't use eggs with bloodspots!

- An egg could have a spot of blood in it. Even a tiny one means the egg is not kosher and should not be used. Some cooks open the egg, put it into a clear glass or bowl and then look at the yolk from all sides.

Equipment

These items pictured are the tools that you will see on equipment lists throughout the book. Use it as a handy reference so you know what items you are looking for in your kitchen before you begin each recipe.

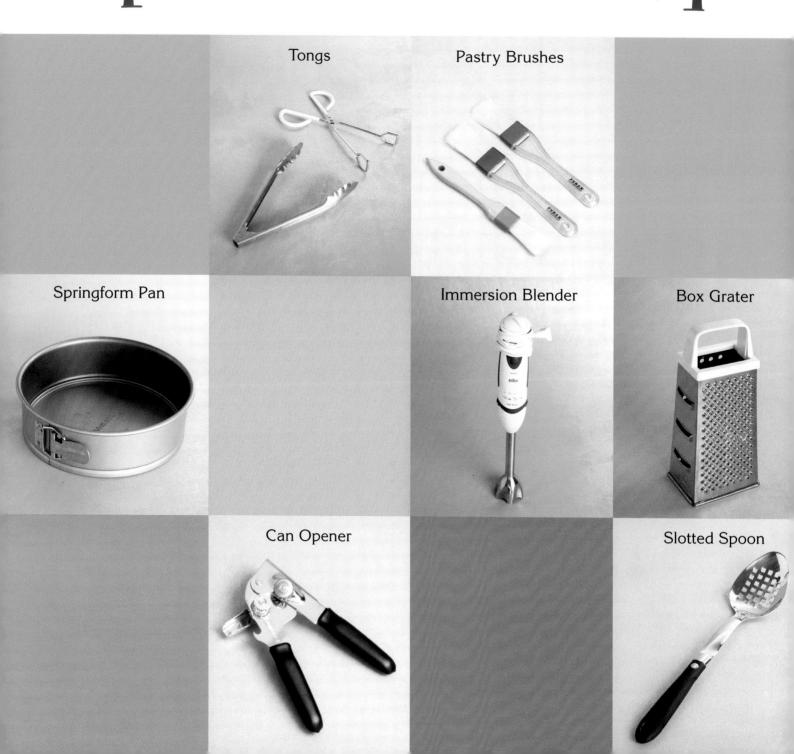

Tongs

Pastry Brushes

Springform Pan

Immersion Blender

Box Grater

Can Opener

Slotted Spoon

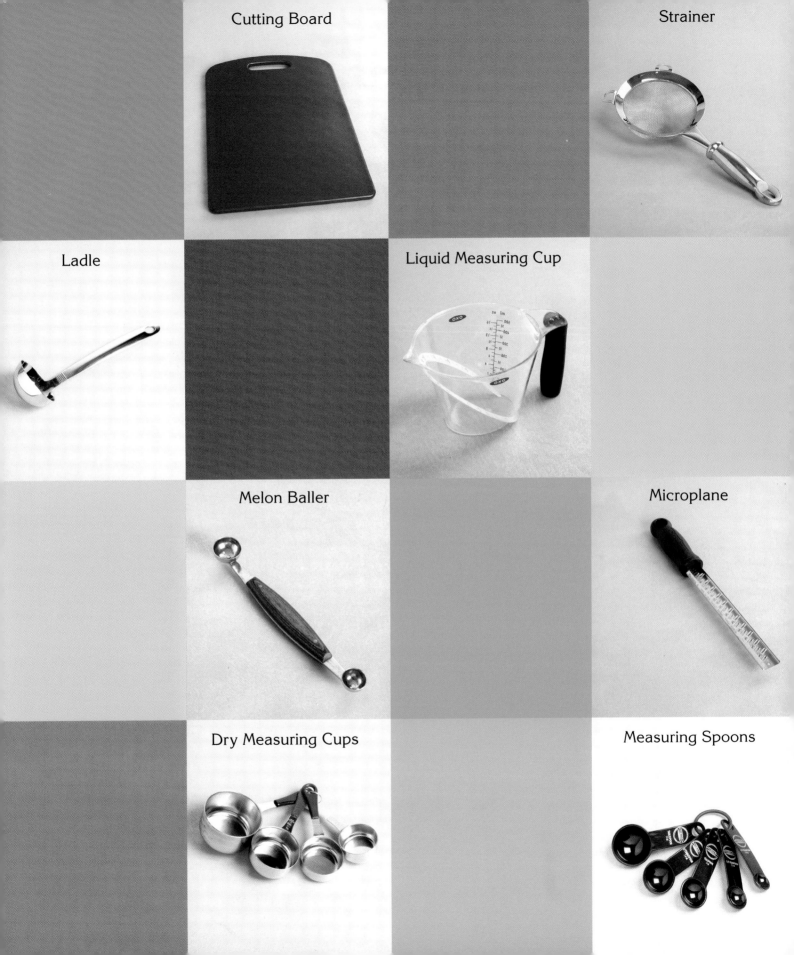

Cutting Board

Strainer

Ladle

Liquid Measuring Cup

Melon Baller

Microplane

Dry Measuring Cups

Measuring Spoons

Whisk

Vegetable Peelers

Offset Spatulas

Potato Masher

Peppermill

Silicone Spatulas

Sifter

Mixing Bowls

Cookie Cutters

Food Processor

Electric Mixer

Ice Cream Scooper

Wooden Spoons

Blender

Rolling Pin

Starters

Saucy Franks

Equipment list:

- scissors
- medium pot
- skinny spatula or spoon
- measuring spoons
- toothpicks or skewers

Ingredient list:

- 1 pound of mini cocktail franks or 6 regular hot dogs, cut into 1-inch pieces
- 1 (12-ounce) jar red currant jelly
- 4 tablespoons spicy brown mustard

You can serve these on toothpicks or pretty skewers.

1. With a pair of scissors, cut open the package of hot dogs. Place the mini franks or sliced hot dogs into the pot.

2. Empty the jar of red currant jelly into the pot. Use your skinny spatula or spoon to get the jelly out of the bottom of the jar.

3. Add the mustard.

4. Turn the heat to medium. Cook the hot dogs uncovered for 15-20 minutes, stirring to mix them with the sauce.

Makes: 6-8 servings

Potato Bourekas

Parve

Equipment list:

- cookie sheet
- parchment paper
- vegetable peeler
- cutting board
- sharp knife
- medium pot
- measuring spoons
- fork
- strainer
- potato masher
- rolling pin
- small bowl
- pastry brush

Ingredient list:

- 1 sheet of puff pastry from a 17.3 ounce box
- 3 Russet potatoes
- 1 teaspoon salt
- 2 tablespoons margarine
- 2 tablespoons soymilk
- ¼ teaspoon freshly ground black pepper
- salt
- 2 large eggs
- 2 tablespoons sesame seeds

These bourekas are great right out of the oven and served with mustard.

1. Preheat the oven to 400° F. Cover the cookie sheet with a piece of parchment paper. Set aside.

2. Open the package of puff pastry. Remove one of the pastry sheets and place it on your counter to thaw. Return the other sheet to the freezer for another use.

3. With your vegetable peeler, peel off and discard the skin of the potatoes. On your cutting board with a sharp knife, cut the potatoes into medium-sized chunks. Place the potato chunks into a medium pot. Add water to cover by 2-3 inches. Add 1 teaspoon of salt to the pot. Over medium heat, bring the water to a boil. Cook the potatoes uncovered until they are soft when you pierce them with a fork. This should take about 25-30 minutes.

4. Place a strainer into the sink. When the potatoes are done, pour them into the strainer, draining out the cooking liquid. Transfer the potatoes back into the pot. Add the margarine, soymilk, black pepper, and salt to taste. Using a potato masher, mash the potatoes. Add one egg to the potatoes and mash until they are light and fluffy. Taste them and see if they need more salt or pepper.

5. With a rolling pin, roll the puff pastry sheet into a large square. With a knife, cut the puff pastry like a tic-tac-toe board into 9 equal squares.

6. Place 1-2 tablespoons of potato filling into the center of each puff pastry square. Fold each

square in half to form a triangle. Press the edges to seal each one. As they are done, place them on the prepared cookie sheet.

7. Crack the second egg into a small bowl. Whisk it with a fork. With a pastry brush, brush the top of each boureka with the beaten egg. Sprinkle the top of each boureka with sesame seeds.

8. Place into the hot oven and bake for 25 minutes, until puffed and golden. Serve warm.

Makes: 9 bourekas

Meatballs 2 Ways

Both of these meatball recipes are great. My kids make 1 batch of meat, split it in half and cook half in each kind of sauce. The meat mixture is exactly the same and the sauce is enough to cover ½ pound of meatballs each. You can try both, or if you like one more than the other, just double the sauce and use the whole batch of meat.

Equipment list:

- medium mixing bowl
- latex glove or large Ziploc® bag
- measuring cups and spoons
- can opener
- 1-2 medium pots with lids
- mixing spoon

Ingredient list:

- 1 pound ground beef
- ¼ cup flavored dry breadcrumbs
- 1 teaspoon onion powder
- 1 large egg

Red Sauce:
- 1 (16-ounce) can of whole berry cranberry sauce
- 1 (26-ounce) jar of your favorite marinara sauce

Brown Sauce:
- ¾ cup dark brown sugar
- 3 tablespoons all-purpose flour
- 1¾ cups water
- ¼ cup white vinegar
- 3 tablespoons soy sauce

1. Place the ground beef into the mixing bowl. Add the breadcrumbs and onion powder. Crack the egg and add it to the bowl. Place the glove or Ziploc® bag over your hand and mush the mixture with your hand until it is all combined.

2. To make the red sauce, use your can opener to open the can of cranberry sauce and the jar of marinara sauce and empty both into a medium pot. Place over medium heat and cook for 5 minutes, stirring with a spoon every few minutes.

3. Roll half of the meatball mixture into balls, the size of large marbles, and carefully add them to the pot. Set the heat as low as possible. Cover the pot and cook for 40 minutes.

4. To make the brown sauce, place the brown sugar, flour, water, vinegar, and soy sauce into a medium pot. Mix to dissolve the flour. Place over medium heat and cook for 3 minutes, stirring with a spoon every few minutes.

5. Roll the other half of the meatball mixture into balls, the size of large marbles, and carefully add them to the pot. Set the heat as low as possible. Cover the pot and cook for 40 minutes.

Makes: 8 servings

Tortilla Fruit Cups

Dairy or Parve

Equipment list:

- measuring cups and spoons
- small bowl
- spoon
- aluminum foil
- paper towel
- microwave
- muffin tin
- cutting board
- sharp knife
- medium mixing bowl
- wooden spoon or silicone spatula

Ingredient list:

- 4 tablespoons sugar
- 2 teaspoons cinnamon
- 6 (6-inch) soft flour tortillas
- nonstick cooking spray, like Pam®
- 1 cup grapes
- 1 ripe banana (make sure it is yellow and firm, not brown and mushy)
- 8 strawberries
- ½ cup fresh blueberries
- ½ cup of strawberry yogurt or non-dairy whipped cream

This pretty and healthy appetizer is so easy to make. The tortilla cups look like beautiful flowers and you can add any fruits or berries that you like to the filling.

1. Preheat the oven to 350° F.

2. Place the sugar and cinnamon into a small bowl. Stir with a spoon until it is all mixed.

3. Lay the tortillas in front of you on big sheets of aluminum foil; this will protect your counters when you use the cooking spray. Spray the tortillas with an even coating of the nonstick spray. Sprinkle with half the cinnamon and sugar. Turn the tortillas over and repeat this on the other side.

4. Transfer each tortilla to a sheet of paper towel and place into the microwave. Microwave on high for 10-12 seconds; this will help soften the tortillas so you can fold them easier into the muffin cups.

5. Spray the cups of the muffin tin with nonstick cooking spray. Place each tortilla into a cup of the muffin tray, folding the sides as you need to get it to fit. The tortillas will stick up over the tray. Put a few tablespoons of water into any empty muffin tins so they don't burn.

6. Place into the oven and bake the tortilla cups for 8-10 minutes, until golden brown.

7. Carefully remove the tray from the oven and cool for 5 minutes. Remove the cups and let them cool all the way. You can make them in advance and keep them in a Ziploc® bag for 2-3 days.

8. Wash and dry all of the fruit.

9. On your cutting board, with a sharp knife, cut the grapes in half. Place them into your medium bowl. Peel the banana. Slice it and then cut each slice in half and add the pieces to the bowl. Trim the stems off the strawberries. Cut the strawberries in half, and then in half again, and add them to the bowl. Place the blueberries into the bowl. Add the yogurt or whipped cream to the bowl and mix gently. Try not to mash the fruit.

10. Scoop some of the fruit into each of the tortilla cups.

Makes: 6 servings

Vegetable Dumplings

Parve

Equipment list:

- food processor
- cutting board
- sharp knife
- measuring cups and spoons
- parchment paper
- cookie sheet
- large pot
- slotted spoon
- large nonstick frying pan (10-14 inches)
- metal spatula

Ingredient list:

- 1 cup thinly sliced Napa or Chinese cabbage
- 4 shiitake mushrooms
- 1 scallion
- 4 baby carrots, or 1 regular carrot cut into 4 pieces
- 1 tablespoon teriyaki sauce
- ¼ teaspoon ground ginger
- ¼ teaspoon salt plus extra
- ½ teaspoon roasted or toasted sesame oil
- 15 (3-4 inch square) wonton wrappers
- 4 tablespoons canola oil
- teriyaki sauce for dipping

1. Place the sliced cabbage into the bowl of a food processor fitted with the metal blade. Remove the stems from the shiitake mushrooms and discard them. Add the shiitake mushroom caps to the bowl of the food processor.

2. On your cutting board, with the sharp knife, slice off the hairy root from the scallion, leaving the white part. Slice off the top half of the remaining scallion and throw out the top green part. Add the white part and the remaining green part to the food processor bowl. Add the carrots. Lock the lid of the food processor and pulse to finely chop the vegetables.

3. Open the lid and add the teriyaki sauce, ginger, ¼ teaspoon salt, and sesame oil to the bowl. Lock the lid and pulse to combine all of the ingredients together.

4. Fill a large pot halfway with water. Add 1 tablespoon of salt. Place it over medium-high heat and let it come to a boil.

5. Meanwhile, lay the wonton wrappers in front of you, four at a time.

6. Fill a small measuring cup with water. Dip your finger into the water and go around the whole outside of each wonton wrapper to wet all 4 edges of each wrapper. Place 1 teaspoonful of the vegetable filling into the center of each wonton wrapper. Fold the wrapper in half on the diagonal to form a triangle. Press around the filling to push out any extra air. Firmly press the edges to seal each wonton. Lay the finished wontons in a single layer on a cookie sheet that is lined with a piece of parchment paper. Make sure they don't touch or they will stick together.

7. Repeat this until all 15 wonton wrappers are filled.

8. Drop the dumplings into the water a few at a time and cook for 1 minute; they will float to the top. Remove the dumplings and place them back on the cookie sheet. Do this until all of the dumplings are done.

9. Pour the 4 tablespoons of canola oil into a large nonstick frying pan. Heat the oil over medium heat. Place a single layer of the dumplings into the pan and cook for 2-3 minutes, until golden brown on one side. Use a metal spatula to flip and fry on the other side. Remove the dumplings as they are done and place on the serving plate. Continue until all of the dumplings are done.

10. Serve with dipping bowls filled with teriyaki sauce.

Makes: 5 servings

Alphabet Soup

Equipment list:

- cutting board
- sharp knife
- measuring cups and spoons
- large pot with lid
- can opener
- ladle

Ingredient list:

- 1 small onion
- 4 garlic cloves
- 2 tablespoons olive oil
- 2 cups crushed canned tomatoes
- 6 cups chicken stock
- ¼ teaspoon dried basil
- ¼ teaspoon dried oregano
- ¼ teaspoon dried thyme
- ¼ teaspoon black pepper
- 1 cup frozen green beans
- 1 cup frozen corn kernels
- 1 cup alphabet pasta, uncooked

1. On the cutting board, use the sharp knife to chop the onions into small pieces. Set aside. Chop the garlic cloves. Set aside.

2. Place the olive oil into a large soup pot and heat over medium.

3. Add the onions to the pot. Turn the heat to medium-low. Cook the onions, stirring them from time to time for 5 minutes. Add the garlic and cook for 2 minutes longer.

4. Use your can opener to open the can of crushed tomatoes. Add the tomatoes and chicken stock to the pot. Sprinkle in the basil, oregano, thyme, and pepper. Add in the frozen green beans and corn kernels. Allow the soup to simmer on medium heat, uncovered, for 20 minutes.

5. Turn off the heat and stir in the pasta. Cover the pot and let it sit for 25-30 minutes (check the package, it is only 20 minutes if the alphabet shapes are egg noodles). Ladle into bowls.

Makes: 6 servings

French Onion Soup with Cheese Toasts

Equipment list:

- cutting board
- sharp knife
- measuring cups and spoons
- large pot
- wooden spoon or silicone spatula
- deep container or bowl
- ovenproof crocks or bowls
- ladle
- baking sheet

Ingredient list:

- 3 onions
- 3 tablespoons butter
- 1 tablespoon olive oil
- 2 tablespoons all-purpose flour
- 4 cups water
- 4 teaspoons parve beef bouillon powder
- ½ teaspoon dried thyme
- ½ teaspoon black pepper
- salt to taste
- 4 (1-inch thick) slices of Italian or French baguette
- 1 cup shredded mozzarella

If you don't have oven-safe crocks, you can make the cheese toasts by topping the baguette slices with the shredded cheese and toasting them in a toaster oven or in the oven under the broiler. When the cheese is melted, remove from the oven and float a cheese toast in each bowl of soup.

1. On the cutting board, use the sharp knife to cut each onion in half, and then slice the onions into thin semi-circles. Set aside.

2. Place the butter and olive oil into a large pot.

3. Turn the heat to medium. When the butter melts, add the onions and cook them, uncovered, for 30 minutes until they are very soft and golden brown. Stir them often to make sure they are not getting too brown or are burning. If they are, lower the heat.

4. Sprinkle the flour into the onions and stir to coat the onions.

5. Pour the water into a deep container or bowl. Add the parve beef bouillon powder, thyme, and black pepper. Mix to dissolve the powder. Carefully pour this stock into the pot of onions.

6. Turn the heat to medium and cook, uncovered, for 20 minutes, stirring after 10 minutes. Taste and add salt if it needs it.

7. Preheat the oven to broil.

8. When the soup is done, carefully ladle it into 4 ovenproof crocks or bowls.

9. Float a slice of bread on top of each bowl. Sprinkle the cheese evenly over the bowls. Place the crocks or bowls onto a baking sheet.

10. Place the tray with the bowls on it into the oven on the middle rack, and broil until the cheese is melted and bubbling, about 2 minutes.

11. Carefully remove the tray from the oven and remind everyone that the bowls will be hot.

Makes: 4 servings

Creamy Broccoli Cauliflower Soup

Dairy or Parve

Equipment list:

- cutting board
- sharp knife
- vegetable peeler
- measuring cups and spoons
- large soup pot with lid
- silicone spatula or wooden spoon
- immersion blender or blender
- spoon
- ladle

Ingredient list:

- ½ large onion
- 1 clove garlic
- 1 shallot
- 1 small Russet potato
- 4 tablespoons butter or margarine
- 6 ounces fresh broccoli florets, about 4 cups
- 6 ounces fresh cauliflower florets, about 4 cups
- 4 cups vegetable broth or chicken stock
- ½ cup light cream or soymilk

Sometimes I buy the broccoli and cauliflower already cut into florets. They sell them in bags at the supermarket in the salad section. If you buy the whole stalk, you will need to cut the florets off of a medium bunch of broccoli and cut the florets off of one head of cauliflower. You can save the broccoli stalks and cook them in boiling water. I like to chop them and toss them with pasta and melted Cheddar cheese.

An immersion blender is a stick blender. It is so useful. It will let you purée the soup right in the pot instead of pouring it into a blender. If you don't have one, wait for the soup to cool to make pouring into the blender less dangerous.

1. On your cutting board, with a sharp knife, remove the papery skin from your onion. Chop your onion half into small ½ inch pieces. Chop the garlic clove and slice the shallot into thin rings. Set them all aside.

2. With your vegetable peeler, peel the skin off of the potato. On your cutting board, with a sharp knife, cut the potato into 1-inch chunks. Set the potato pieces aside.

3. Place your butter or margarine into the large pot.

4. Melt the butter or margarine over medium heat.

5. Add the chopped onion, garlic, and shallots. Cook for 6 minutes, stirring with a wooden spoon or silicone spatula. The onions will get shiny and golden. If they start to burn, lower the flame immediately.

6. Add the potato pieces, broccoli florets, and cauliflower florets to the pot.

7. Add the vegetable broth or chicken stock to the pot.

8. Cover the pot and cook the soup for 25-30 minutes, until the vegetables are soft.

9. Uncover the pot and turn off the heat. With an immersion blender, purée the soup until it is smooth and creamy, about 3 full minutes.

10. Carefully use a spoon to taste the soup and add salt if it needs it.

11. Add the light cream or soy milk and purée for 1 more minute.

12. Ladle into bowls.

Makes: 6 servings

Strawberry Blueberry Swirl Soup

Dairy

Equipment list:

- measuring cups and spoons
- food processor or blender
- silicone or rubber spatula
- 3 medium mixing bowls
- small mesh strainer
- whisk
- 2 teacups
- serving bowls
- fork

Ingredient list:

Strawberry Soup:

- 2 cups fresh strawberries, cut in quarters
- 1 cup vanilla yogurt
- ½ cup buttermilk or sour cream
- 1 teaspoon pure vanilla extract
- 3 tablespoons sugar

Blueberry Soup:

- 1 cup fresh blueberries
- 1 cup vanilla yogurt
- ½ cup buttermilk or sour cream
- 1 teaspoon pure vanilla extract
- 3 tablespoons sugar

1. Place the strawberries, yogurt, buttermilk or sour cream, vanilla, and sugar into the bowl of a food processor fitted with a metal blade or blender.

2. Cover the food processor or blender with the lid and blend for 1 minute until the mixture is smooth. Turn off the machine.

3. Pour the strawberry soup into a medium bowl. Use the spatula to get all of the soup out of the food processor or blender. Set aside.

4. Carefully rinse out the food processor or blender. Put it back together on the base.

5. The blueberry soup is made a little differently in order to keep the blueberry skins out of the soup. Place the blueberries into the food processor or blender. Pulse until smooth.

6. Place a small mesh strainer over a medium bowl. Using a silicone or rubber spatula, scoop out the blueberries and put them into the strainer. Press with the spatula to get the juice out of the blueberries. Discard the skins.

7. To the strained blueberries in the bowl add the yogurt, buttermilk or sour cream, vanilla, and sugar. Whisk to combine.

8. To serve, take 2 teacups. Fill 1 cup with the strawberry soup and 1 cup with the blueberry soup. At the same time, pour them into a bowl so that they meet in the middle. With the tines of a fork, swirl the two soups together.

 akes: 4 servings

Mini Meatball Soup

Meat

Equipment list:

- measuring cups and spoons
- large pot with lid
- medium bowl
- garlic press
- latex glove or Ziploc® bag
- cutting board
- sharp knife
- spoon
- ladle

Ingredient list:

- 6 cups chicken stock
- ½ pound ground beef
- ⅛ cup seasoned bread crumbs
- ¼ teaspoon dried oregano
- 2 garlic cloves
- 30 fresh baby spinach leaves
- 5 fresh basil leaves
- salt
- black pepper

1. Pour the chicken stock into a large pot.

2. Over medium heat, bring the stock to a boil. Turn the heat down to a low simmer.

3. Place the ground beef into a medium bowl. Add the bread crumbs and oregano. With a garlic press, mince the garlic into the bowl. Cover your hand with a latex glove or Ziploc® bag. With that hand, knead lightly to mix, but don't over-mix it or the meatballs will be tough.

4. Roll the meat mixture into mini meatballs, the size of large marbles. Handle as little as possible or the meatballs will be tough when they are cooked.

5. Carefully drop the meatballs into the barely simmering chicken stock.

6. Cook, covered, for 8 minutes.

7. Wash your hands and anything that the raw meat touched.

8. On the cutting board, with a sharp knife, make a stack of the spinach leaves. Slice into thin ribbons. Do the same thing with the basil leaves.

9. Add the sliced spinach and basil to the pot.

10. Simmer for another 10 minutes, uncovered.

11. Use a spoon to taste the soup. Add salt and freshly ground black pepper until it tastes good to you.

12. Ladle into bowls.

Makes: 6 servings

Asian Wonton Soup

Equipment list:

- garlic press
- medium mixing bowl
- cutting board
- sharp knife
- measuring cups and spoons
- parchment paper
- medium pot with lid
- long handled wooden spoon

Ingredient list:

Wontons:

- 4 ounces ground chicken
- ¼ teaspoon ground ginger
- 2 cloves garlic, minced
- 1 tablespoon teriyaki sauce
- ¼ teaspoon salt
- ¼ teaspoon black pepper
- 12 (3 or 4-inch square) wonton wrappers

Soup:

- 8 shiitake mushrooms
- 1 tablespoon canola oil
- 1 small head of Napa cabbage
- 6 cups chicken stock
- ¼ teaspoon black pepper
- 2 scallions
- 1 teaspoon roasted or toasted sesame oil

If you don't have ground chicken, put one raw chicken cutlet into a food processor and pulse until ground.

1. Place the ground chicken, ginger, minced garlic cloves, teriyaki sauce, salt, and pepper into a medium bowl. Mix well. If you have a latex glove, put it on and use your hand to really mush the ingredients together.

2. Lay the wonton wrappers in front of you, four at a time.

3. Fill a small measuring cup with water. Dip your finger into the water and go around the whole outside of each wonton wrapper to wet all 4 edges of each wrapper. Place 1 teaspoonful of the chicken filling into the center of each wonton wrapper. Fold the wrapper in half on the diagonal to form a triangle. Press around the filling to push out any extra air. Firmly press the edges to seal each wonton.

4. Repeat this until all 12 wonton wrappers are filled. If you end up with extra filling, simply freeze it for another time. Lay the finished wontons on a piece of parchment paper in a single layer. Make sure they don't touch or they will stick together.

5. Wash your hands and anything that the chicken touched with warm soapy water.

6. Pull the stems off of the 8 shiitake mushrooms and throw the stems out. On your cutting board, with a sharp knife, slice the shiitake mushroom caps.

7. Place the canola oil in the medium pot. Get the oil hot over medium-low heat. Add the mushrooms. Cook for 5 minutes, until the mushrooms are soft,

a little brown and smell good. It is okay if the mushrooms give off a little liquid, they will do this before they turn brown. You can stir them with your wooden spoon as they cook to make sure they are not sticking to the pot.

8. On your cutting board, with a sharp knife, slice some of the Napa cabbage. Measure 1 loose cup of it and carefully add it to the pot. Cook for 2 minutes, until the cabbage is wilted.

9. Add the chicken stock to the pot. Add in the pepper.

10. When the soup starts to simmer, carefully add the wontons into the soup. Cover the pot and cook for 4 minutes. The wontons are done when they float to the top of the pot.

11. On your cutting board, with the sharp knife, slice off the hairy root from the scallions, leaving the white part. Slice off the top half of the remaining scallion and throw out the top green part. Thinly slice the white part and the remaining green part. Sprinkle the scallions into the soup. Carefully add the sesame oil. Stir one time. Ladle into bowls.

Makes: 4-6 servings

Caesar Salad

Equipment list:

- paper towels
- large salad bowl
- measuring cups and spoons
- food processor or blender
- 2 large spoons for tossing salad

Ingredient list:

- 1 head Romaine lettuce
- ⅓ cup extra virgin olive oil
- ¼ cup mayonnaise
- 2 tablespoons red wine vinegar
- 1 teaspoon Worcestershire sauce
- ½ teaspoon salt
- ¼ teaspoon dry mustard powder
- 1 teaspoon Dijon mustard
- 2 tablespoons sour cream or plain yogurt
- 2 garlic cloves
- ½ lemon
- ⅓ cup Parmesan cheese
- 1 cup croutons

1. Separate the romaine lettuce leaves. Rinse them and pat them dry well with paper towels. Tear the lettuce leaves into bite-sized pieces and place them into a large salad bowl.

2. Place the olive oil, mayonnaise, red wine vinegar, Worcestershire sauce, salt, mustard powder, Dijon mustard, sour cream or yogurt, and garlic into the bowl of a food processor fitted with a metal blade or into a blender. Pulse to blend all of the ingredients.

3. Pour the dressing over the lettuce. Toss with 2 large spoons to combine. Place the lemon half in your hand. Squeeze it over the salad, letting the juice run through your fingers but catching the pits. Throw the pits away.

4. Sprinkle the Parmesan cheese over the salad. Toss in the croutons.

Makes: 6 servings

Veggies with Ranch Dip

Dairy

Equipment list:
- medium mixing bowl
- measuring cups and spoons
- scissors
- whisk
- cutting board
- sharp knife
- mini cookie cutters, optional
- vegetable peeler
- toothpicks and ramekins

Ingredient list:
- ¼ cup mayonnaise
- ½ cup sour cream
- 1½ teaspoons white vinegar
- 3-4 stems of fresh parsley
- 3-4 stems of fresh dill
- ½ teaspoon garlic powder
- ¼ teaspoon onion powder
- ¼ teaspoon salt
- ¼ teaspoon black pepper
- 1 red bell pepper
- 1 green bell pepper
- 2 small cucumbers
- 2 stalks celery
- 1 cup cherry or grape tomatoes
- 1 cup baby carrots

1. In a medium bowl, place the mayonnaise, sour cream, and vinegar.

2. With clean scissors, snip off 1 tablespoon of fresh parsley leaves and 1 tablespoon of fresh dill. Add them to the bowl.

3. Sprinkle in the garlic powder, onion powder, salt, and pepper. Whisk to combine it all together.

4. You can make this in advance and keep it in the bowl, covered, in the refrigerator.

5. Wash and dry the red and green peppers.

6. On your cutting board, with a sharp knife, cut the red and green peppers in half. Scoop out the seeds and stem and throw them out. Slice the peppers into strips or use mini cookie cutters to cut them into fun shapes.

7. Wash the cucumbers. Peel them with the vegetable peeler and throw out the skin. On your cutting board, with a sharp knife, cut them into rounds or spears. Wash the celery, and slice off the root and the top part. Discard them. Cut the celery into chunks.

8. Spear all of the cut vegetables along with the tomatoes and baby carrots on fun toothpicks or skewers or display them in ramekins. Serve with the dip.

Makes: 6 servings

Rainbow Salad

Parve

Equipment list:

- cutting board
- sharp knife
- medium mixing bowl
- can opener
- vegetable peeler
- measuring cups and spoons
- small bowl or container
- whisk

Ingredient list:

- 1 red bell pepper
- 1 yellow bell pepper
- 1 (15-ounce) can of baby corn
- 1 cup snow peas or sugar snap peas
- 1 carrot
- 10 green beans
- ½ red onion
- ¼ cup sugar
- ⅓ cup apple cider vinegar or balsamic vinegar
- ¼ teaspoon salt
- ⅛ teaspoon black pepper
- ⅛ cup olive oil
- ¼ teaspoon garlic powder

This is a fun, colorful mix of vegetables. In a pinch, you can use bottled Italian dressing.

1. On your cutting board, with a sharp knife, cut the red and yellow peppers in half. Scoop out the seeds and stems and throw them out. Slice the peppers into thin strips. Place them into the bowl.

2. Using your can opener, open the can of baby corn, drain it, and add the corn to the bowl.

3. Wash and dry the snow peas and add them to the bowl.

4. Using your vegetable peeler, peel the carrot. Slice it into skinny discs and add them to the bowl.

5. Wash and dry the green beans. Snap off and discard the ends of the green beans. Add the green beans to the bowl.

6. Remove the papery skin from the red onion. On your cutting board, with a sharp knife, slice the onion into very thin strips. Place them into the bowl.

7. Place the sugar, vinegar, salt, pepper, olive oil, and garlic powder into a small bowl. Whisk it all together. You could also just put these ingredients into a container with a lid and give it a few good shakes, until the dressing is all mixed. Pour the dressing over the vegetables and let them sit in the dressing for 1 hour or up to 4 hours before serving.

Makes: 4 servings

Breakfast

Egg in a Frame

Equipment list:

- medium round or heart shaped cookie cutter
- large frying pan with lid
- measuring cups and spoons
- spatula

Ingredient list:

- 4 slices white bread
- 4 tablespoons butter
- 4 medium eggs, divided

This is a fun variation on sunny-side-up eggs with a side order of toast. You can use almost any shape cookie cutters, just make sure that the hole it makes is big enough for the whole egg to fit into but still leaves some bread as the frame.

1. Lay 1 slice of white bread in front of you. Place your cookie cutter in the center of the piece of bread. When you have it perfectly centered, press down and cut out the shape. Do this with all 4 pieces, being careful not to break the frame of crust. Place the cutout shapes aside for another use, such as the Hearty Blintzes on page 50.

2. Prepare the eggs. Crack each egg into a small measuring cup; make sure the yolk stays whole. Set aside.

3. Place the butter into a large frying pan over medium-low heat.

4. When the butter melts, add the bread. Cook for 1-2 minutes and then turn each piece of bread over. The bread should be golden brown.

5. Slowly pour an egg into the hole in each slice of bread. Cook until the eggs are set. You can cover the pan with a lid to help the top of the egg set. Remove from heat.

6. Slide your spatula under each egg and frame and move them to the serving plates.

Makes: 4 servings

Goldilox

Equipment list:

- medium mixing bowl
- whisk
- small frying pan
- wooden spoon or silicone spatula

Ingredient list:

- 4 large eggs
- 4 tablespoons milk
- 2 tablespoons butter
- 4 tablespoons cream cheese, block cream cheese (not whipped)
- 1-2 slices of lox
- fresh dill for garnish

Many times after your family has a Sunday brunch there will be a little leftover lox. This funky version of scrambled eggs is a great way to use it up.

1. Crack the eggs into a medium bowl. Add the milk. Whisk the eggs until they are mixed and a little foamy.

2. Place the butter into the frying pan and melt it over medium heat.

3. When the butter is melted, pour in the egg mixture.

4. With your fingertips, break the cream cheese up into 4-5 small chunks. Add them to the eggs.

5. With your fingers, rip the piece of lox into small strips and add them to the pan.

6. Using a wooden spoon or silicone spatula, mix the eggs with the cream cheese and lox until they are perfectly scrambled, fluffy, and bright yellow.

7. Transfer the eggs to a plate.

8. Garnish with a sprig of fresh dill.

Makes: 1-2 servings

Hearty Blintzes

Equipment list:

- cookie sheet
- parchment paper
- measuring spoons
- medium mixing bowl
- electric mixer
- heart or round cookie cutters
- fork
- small microwave-safe bowl
- microwave
- spoon
- pastry brush

Ingredient list:

- 1 (3-ounce) package cream cheese (not whipped)
- 1 egg yolk
- 1 tablespoon sugar
- 20 pieces of fresh white bread
- optional: blueberries, sliced strawberries
- 6 tablespoons butter
- 1 teaspoon cinnamon
- 3 teaspoons sugar

1. Preheat the oven to 400° F.

2. Line the cookie sheet with parchment paper. Set aside.

3. In a mixing bowl, with an electric mixture at medium speed, beat the cream cheese with the egg yolk and sugar until it is smooth and creamy. Set aside.

4. With your heart or round cookie cutter, cut the shape out of the center of each piece of white bread one at a time. Throw away the crusts.

5. Place a heaping teaspoon or two of the cream cheese mixture in the center of 10 of the bread shapes.

6. You can leave them plain or top them with a few blueberries or a slice of strawberry. Cover each with a second bread heart or circle.

7. With your fingers, go around the very edges of the "sandwich" to pinch the two pieces of bread together. Do the same thing with the tines of your fork facing into the bread. Go around the edges to give a pretty edge and to firmly seal the seams. Place the blintze sandwiches on the prepared cookie sheet.

8. Place the butter into a small microwave-safe bowl and microwave for 45 seconds, or until it melts.

9. Carefully remove the bowl of butter and use a spoon to stir in the cinnamon and 3 teaspoons of sugar.

10. Using your pastry brush, carefully brush both sides of the "sandwich" with the butter/cinnamon mixture. Be generous, really brush it on.

11. Place into the oven and bake for 10 minutes.

12. Carefully remove from oven and allow to cool for a few minutes.

Makes: 10 blintzes

Unreal Oatmeal

Equipment list:

- measuring cups and spoons
- medium pot
- wooden spoon

I can still remember my little girls starting every single morning with a bowl of this oatmeal. My husband would tell them Goldilocks and the Three Bears, and with grateful faces and little voices they would tell me, "Das goood mama". Eight years later, it is still the way they start their day only now they make it themselves!

For a unique crunchy topping, sprinkle some of the granola from page (70).

Ingredient list:

- 1 cup old fashioned rolled oats (not instant or quick cooking type)
- 1 cup whole or 2% milk
- 1 cup water
- 1 teaspoon butter
- ¼ teaspoon coarse or kosher salt
- 2 teaspoons heavy cream
- 2 tablespoons maple syrup, divided
- raisins, optional

1. Place the oats, milk, and water into a medium pot.

2. Turn the heat to medium. Cook for 8-10 minutes, uncovered, stirring as it thickens and cooks.

3. Once the oatmeal is creamy, add the butter and salt. Mix in and remove from the heat.

4. Stir in the heavy cream.

5. Spoon the oatmeal into 2 bowls.

6. Drizzle a circle of 1 tablespoon maple syrup around each bowl. If desired, toss in some raisins or arrange them in the shape of a smiley face.

Makes: 2 servings

Healthy Banana Splits

Equipment list:

- cutting board
- knife
- measuring cups and spoons
- ice cream scooper
- bowls or glasses
- can opener

Ingredient list:

- 1 medium banana
- ½ cup cottage cheese
- 3 strawberries
- 5-6 blueberries
- 3 tablespoons crushed pineapple, from a small can

All the fun of a banana split but healthy enough for breakfast!

1. Peel the banana and place it on your cutting board.

2. With your knife, split the banana lengthwise, and then cut each half again lengthwise. You will end up with 4 long spears.

3. Place the bananas in the bowl or glass, letting the 4 spears touch in the middle.

4. Using your ice cream scooper, add a scoop of cottage cheese to the center of your bowl or glass.

5. Place the strawberries on your cutting board and with your knife chop them into small pieces.

6. Toss the strawberries over the cottage cheese. Add the blueberries.

7. With a can opener, open the crushed pineapple. Drizzle 3 tablespoons of the crushed pineapple over the top.

Makes: 1 serving

Banana Berry Bread

Dairy

Equipment list:

- 9-inch loaf pan
- measuring cups and spoons
- electric mixer and bowl
- wooden spoon or silicone spatula
- cookie sheet
- knife
- wire rack

Ingredient list:

- nonstick cooking spray, like Pam®
- ½ cup (1 stick) butter
- 1½ cups sugar
- 2 large eggs
- ½ cup sour cream
- 1 teaspoon pure vanilla extract
- 1½ cups mashed ripe bananas (3-4 medium bananas)
- 2½ cups all-purpose flour
- 1 teaspoon baking soda
- 1 teaspoon salt
- 1 cup fresh or frozen blueberries

1. Make sure there is a rack in the center of the oven and none above it to give room for the banana bread to grow. Preheat the oven to 350° F.

2. Spray the bottom of the loaf pan with nonstick cooking spray. Try not to get too much spray on the sides; this will help the banana bread to rise nicely.

3. Either leave the stick of butter on the counter for 15 minutes to soften at room temperature, or place it in the microwave and microwave it for 15 seconds.

4. In the bowl of a mixer, mix the butter, sugar, and eggs until they are light and creamy. Add the sour cream, vanilla, and mashed bananas. Mix until all combined.

5. Sprinkle in the flour, baking soda, and salt. Mix until just combined; it will be thick and sticky.

6. With a wooden spoon or silicone spatula, stir in the blueberries trying not to mush them.

7. Pour the batter into the loaf pan. Place the loaf pan on a cookie sheet to catch any batter that may overflow as it bakes.

8. Place the cookie sheet with the pan into the hot oven and bake for 1 hour and 15 minutes.

9. Carefully remove and allow the banana berry bread to cool for 5 minutes.

10. Run a knife around the edges to loosen the sides of the bread, turn the bread over and set it on a rack or plate to cool completely.

Makes: 1 loaf

Fluffy Pancakes 3 Ways

Dairy or Parve

Equipment list:

- sifter
- large mixing bowl
- measuring cups and spoons
- wooden spoon
- large frying pan
- metal spatula

Ingredient list:

- 1¾ cups all-purpose flour
- 3½ teaspoons baking powder
- 1 teaspoon salt
- 2 tablespoons sugar
- 1½ cups milk or soymilk
- 2 large eggs
- optional mix ins: ½ cup semi-sweet chocolate chips or ½ cup fresh blueberries
- 3 tablespoons butter or margarine
- pancake or maple syrup

These are the fluffiest pancakes you will ever have. You can make them plain, or add a mix-in of chocolate chips or fresh blueberries.

1. Position a sifter over a large bowl. Pour the flour, baking powder, salt, and sugar into the sifter and sift the ingredients into the large bowl.

2. Pour the milk or soymilk into the bowl. Add the eggs.

3. Using your wooden spoon, mix until mostly smooth; leave some lumps. If you are adding the chocolate chips or blueberries, add them here, stirring to mix them into the batter.

4. Place the butter or margarine into a large frying pan. Turn the heat to medium and allow the butter or margarine to melt.

5. Using a large spoon or the ¼ cup measuring cup, scoop out the batter into the frying pan.

6. When one side is golden brown, flip the pancakes with the spatula.

7. You will need to cook the pancakes in batches. The butter may start to burn after a batch or two. If this happens, turn off the heat and carefully wipe out the pan with a paper towel. Add fresh butter or margarine, allow it to melt and begin cooking the pancakes again.

8. Serve with maple syrup or pancake syrup if desired.

Makes: 9-12 pancakes

Chocolate Croissants

Dairy or Parve

Equipment list:

- kitchen towel
- small mixing bowl
- knife
- cookie sheet
- parchment paper
- pastry brush

Ingredient list:

- ½ (17.5-ounce) box puff pastry dough
- 1 large egg yolk
- 1 tablespoon heavy cream or soymilk
- 2 (3.5 ounce) milk chocolate or semi-sweet chocolate bars
- sugar

These rich delicacies are a real treat at breakfast, brunch or even for dessert. They are so simple to make, which is good because they disappear so quickly, you may need to whip up a spare batch.

1. Preheat the oven to 400° F.

2. Remove the puff pastry from the freezer. Take 1 sheet out of the package and return the second sheet to the freezer. Lightly cover the puff pastry sheet with a kitchen towel and allow it to thaw for 25 minutes on the counter.

3. In a small bowl, mix the egg yolk with the heavy cream or soymilk.

4. Line a cookie sheet with parchment paper. Set aside.

5. Unroll the puff pastry sheet and then cut the puff pastry on the creases into 3 long strips. Cut each strip into 3 equal squares. You will have 9 equal squares.

6. Brush the tops of each square all over with the egg yolk mixture.

7. Place a long rectangle of chocolate down the center of one square. Bring both sides of the puff pastry to the center and pinch the sides together to enclose the chocolate.

8. Place the pastry, seam side down, on the prepared cookie sheet.

9. Do this with all 9 chocolate rectangles and puff pastry squares.

10. Brush the tops of each croissant with the remaining egg yolk mixture. Sprinkle each with a pinch of sugar.

11. Place into the hot oven and bake for 15 minutes, until the croissants are puffed and golden brown.

Makes: 9 croissants

Breakfast Burritos

Dairy

Equipment list:

- medium mixing bowl
- measuring cups and spoons
- whisk
- 8-inch frying pan
- wooden spoon or silicone spatula
- microwave oven
- aluminum foil
- spoons

Ingredient list:

- 4 large eggs
- 2 tablespoons milk
- 1 tablespoon butter
- ½ cup shredded Cheddar cheese
- 2 large (9-10 inch) flour tortillas
- 6 tablespoons bottled salsa

Makes: 2 burritos

If you like a little spice to start your day, then these breakfast burritos are for you! You can control the spiciness with the kind of salsa you use. Go for mild for not spicy and medium or hot for a fiery dish.

1. Crack the eggs into a medium bowl. Add the milk.
2. Using your whisk, mix the eggs and milk, and then beat briskly to get some air into the eggs.
3. Place the butter into the frying pan. Place it over medium heat. When the butter is melted, add the eggs.
4. Using your wooden spoon or silicone spatula, scramble the eggs.
5. When the eggs are a little set, add the shredded Cheddar cheese and mix it in. Cook until the eggs are bright yellow, fluffy, and not runny at all and the cheese is melted.
6. Carefully remove the pan from the heat.
7. Warm the tortillas in the microwave for 15 seconds.
8. Spoon the egg mixture into the center of the tortilla.
9. Spoon the salsa on top of the eggs.
10. Fold two opposite sides of the tortilla to the center. Roll up the tortilla from the bottom. You can leave the top open so the pretty colors of the eggs and salsa show or roll it the whole way.
11. To keep the burritos warm, you can wrap them in aluminum foil and place them into a 350° F oven for 10 minutes.

Crunchy French Toast Sticks

Dairy

Equipment list:

- medium mixing bowl
- whisk
- plate
- cutting board
- sharp knife
- large frying pan
- spatula

Ingredient list:

- 2 large eggs
- 1 tablespoon heavy cream or milk
- ¼ cup cornflake crumbs
- ¼ cup crisp rice cereal like Rice Krispies®
- 2 slices challah or white bread
- 1 tablespoon butter
- pancake or maple syrup

This recipe makes enough for 1 or 2 people. If you want to make it for more, just double the ingredients. When it comes time to cooking the French Toast Sticks, make one batch and then carefully wipe out the pan. Let the pan cool and start by melting fresh butter for a second batch. If you keep reusing the same pan, the old butter will burn.

1. Crack the eggs into a medium bowl. With a whisk, whip the eggs with the heavy cream or milk. Set the bowl aside.

2. Place the cornflake crumbs and crisp rice cereal onto a plate. Blend them together with your fingers.

3. On your cutting board, with a sharp knife, slice each piece of bread into 3 strips.

4. Pick up one of the pieces of bread. Dip it into the egg mixture, coating both sides.

5. Roll it into the cereal mixture, coating it on all sides.

6. Repeat with the other 5 strips of bread.

7. Place the butter into a large frying pan. Turn the heat to low.

8. When the butter is melted, add the 6 french toast sticks.

9. When they are golden brown, flip them over with a spatula.

10. Serve with pancake or maple syrup.

Makes: 6 french toast sticks

Snacks

Baked Nachos

Dairy

Equipment list:

- cookie sheet
- parchment paper
- measuring cups

Ingredient list:

- 1 (12-ounce) bag tortilla chips
- 2 cups shredded Cheddar cheese
- ¼ cup store bought salsa or Salsamolé (facing page)
- ½ cup sour cream
- ¼ cup pitted, sliced black olives (from a small can), optional

Makes: 8 servings

1. Preheat the oven to 400° F.

2. Line the cookie sheet with parchment paper.

3. Empty the chips onto the parchment lined cookie sheet.

4. Sprinkle the cheese all over the chips.

5. Place into the oven and bake for 8-10 minutes, until the cheese is melted.

6. Pour the salsa and sour cream into small bowls. Serve the nachos with the salsa and sour cream or Salsamolé. If you like, you can scatter the olives over the top.

Salsamolé (Salsa Guacamole Combo)

Parve

Equipment list:

- cutting board
- paring knife
- spoon
- medium serving bowl
- fork
- can opener
- sharp knife
- measuring spoons
- garlic press

Ingredient list:

- 2 ripe Hass avocados (black skin)
- 1 (14.5 ounce) can diced tomatoes
- ½ lime
- ½ red onion
- 1 clove garlic
- ½ teaspoon salt
- 4 dashes hot sauce, like Tabasco®
- tortilla chips

1. Place an avocado on your cutting board. With a paring knife, cut it lengthwise in half, starting at the stem end. Cut around the pit that is in the center.

2. Holding the avocado with your hands, gently twist the halves to separate them.

3. Scoop out the pit with your spoon and discard. Scoop out the flesh and place it into the bowl. Repeat with the second avocado.

4. Mash the avocado with a fork until it is almost smooth.

5. With your can opener open the can of tomatoes. Using a fork, remove the tomatoes from the liquid and place them into the bowl. Throw out the liquid.

6. Holding the lime in your hand, squeeze it over the bowl, letting the juice run through your fingers, catch the pits to throw away.

7. Place your ½ red onion on your cutting board. Remove any papery skin. With a sharp knife, chop the onion into tiny pieces. Add them to the bowl.

8. Place the garlic clove into the garlic press. Squeeze the press to mince the garlic into the bowl.

9. Add the salt. Add the hot sauce one shake at a time. Mix and taste to see if you want it hotter.

10. Serve with tortilla chips or the Baked Nachos.

Makes: 8 servings

Granola and Yogurt Sundaes

Dairy

Equipment list:

- large mixing bowl
- measuring cups and spoons
- silicone spatula
- small mixing bowl
- whisk
- baking pan
- parchment paper
- ice cream sundae glasses

Ingredient list:

- 1½ cups old fashioned oats (not instant or quick cooking type)
- ½ cup raw sunflower seeds, shelled, not the roasted type
- ½ cup sweetened dried cranberries, like Craisins®
- ¼ cup chopped pecans
- ¼ cup chopped walnuts
- ¼ cup slivered almonds
- 4 tablespoons dark brown sugar
- 4 tablespoons pure maple syrup (not pancake syrup)
- 1 teaspoon pure vanilla extract
- 2 tablespoons vegetable oil
- ½ teaspoon salt
- 4 cups strawberry or vanilla yogurt
- 1 cup of assorted berries

This granola is so yummy, be sure to make some extra to have as a snack for your lunchbag.

1. Preheat the oven to 350° F.

2. In a large bowl, combine the oats, sunflower seeds, cranberries, pecans, walnuts, and almonds.

3. In a small bowl, with a whisk, combine the brown sugar, maple syrup, vanilla, oil, and salt. Pour this mixture over the oat mixture and toss it with your spatula to combine.

4. Line the baking pan with parchment paper.

5. Pour the oat mixture into the pan. With your silicone spatula, spread into a flat layer.

6. Place the pan into the oven and bake for 15 minutes, stirring once halfway through the cooking time, to help it dry out and keep from burning.

7. Remove from oven and allow to cool. You can even make this in advance and keep it in a heavy duty Ziploc® bag for up to two weeks.

8. Pour ¼ cup of yogurt into each of 4 tall sundae glasses.

9. Top with a 1-inch layer of granola.

10. Pour on another ¼ cup of yogurt.

11. Top with a second layer of granola, a layer of yogurt, a layer of granola, and ending with a layer of yogurt. Sprinkle ¼ cup of the mixed berries on top.

12. Serve each sundae with a long spoon.

M akes: 9 granola and yogurt sundaes

Gourmet Popcorn

E quipment list:

- jelly roll pan
- parchment paper
- small pot
- measuring cups and spoons
- wooden spoon
- electric mixer
- large mixing bowl

I ngredient list:

Spicy-Cheese Popcorn:

- 6 tablespoons butter
- ¾ teaspoon paprika
- ¾ teaspoon onion powder
- ¾ teaspoon chili powder
- ¾ teaspoon garlic powder
- ¾ teaspoon salt
- ⅓ cup grated Parmesan cheese
- 10-12 cups air popped plain popcorn or popped from a microwave bag

Caramel Popcorn:

- 8 tablespoons (1 stick) butter
- ½ cup firmly packed dark brown sugar
- 10-12 cups air popped plain popcorn or popped from a microwave bag

Next time you're planning an at-home family fun night, shake things up a little with these two spins on plain ol' popcorn. The caramel is sweet and crunchy and the cheese is spicy with some kick.

Spicy-Cheese Popcorn:

1. Preheat the oven to 350° F.

2. Cover a jelly roll pan with a sheet of parchment paper. Set aside.

3. Place the butter into a small pot. Add the paprika, onion powder, chili powder, garlic powder, and salt. Turn the heat to medium-low and cook until the butter melts. Mix with a wooden spoon until all the spices are combined.

4. Pour the popped popcorn into a large mixing bowl. Mix in the spice mixture. With a wooden spoon, mix very well to get all of the pieces coated. Sprinkle on the Parmesan cheese and toss to coat.

5. Empty the cheese coated popcorn onto the prepared jelly roll pan. Place into the oven and bake for 7-8 minutes, until crisp.

Caramel Popcorn:

1. Preheat the oven to 350° F.

2. Cover a jelly roll pan with a sheet of parchment paper. Set aside.

3. Take the butter out of the refrigerator and let it sit for 15 minutes to get soft. You can also put it in the microwave for 15 seconds.

4. Place the butter and brown sugar into a large mixing bowl. With an electric mixer, cream the butter and sugar. Whip it until it is fluffy.

5. Add the popped popcorn to the bowl. With a wooden spoon, mix very well to get all of the pieces coated.

6. Empty the coated popcorn onto the prepared jelly roll pan. Place into the oven and bake for 7-8 minutes, until crisp.

Makes: 6 servings per batch

Chocolate Fondue

Dairy

E quipment list:

- microwave-safe bowl
- measuring cups and spoons
- microwave
- whisk
- fondue pot with tea light
- skewers or sticks

I ngredient list:

- 4 ounces good quality semi-sweet chocolate, broken into pieces
- ½ cup heavy cream or light cream
- 2 teaspoons butter
- ½ teaspoon pure vanilla extract
- 1 tablespoon sugar
- Choose from: banana slices, apple chunks, pretzels, vanilla cookies, strawberries, marshmallows

Everything tastes better after being dipped in chocolate. That's what fondue is all about!

For the chocolate, you could use chocolate bars which you can break up with your hands. You can also use chocolate chips. Pop one in your mouth and make sure they are good quality and don't taste waxy.

If you don't have a fondue pot, there is no need to skip this recipe. You will just have to eat what you dip quickly because the chocolate won't stay hot and melted.

If you end up with extra fondue, you can keep it in the refrigerator and just microwave it to warm it up.

Although this recipe is dairy, don't use milk chocolate; it is runnier when it melts and won't coat the items as well.

1. Place your chocolate pieces into a microwave-safe bowl. Add the cream, butter, vanilla, and sugar.

2. Heat it in the microwave for 1 minute.

3. Carefully remove the bowl from the microwave; it will be hot. Whisk the mixture until the chocolate is smooth and creamy.

4. Transfer the fondue to a fondue pot. Carefully light the tea light, which will make your fondue pot just warm enough to keep the chocolate melted.

5. Place your choice of fruits and treats on skewers. Dip into the melted chocolate. Pretzel rods and vanilla cookies can be dipped carefully by hand.

M akes: 1 cup of fondue

30-Second S'mores

Dairy or Parve

Equipment list:

- paper plate or microwave-safe plate
- microwave

Ingredient list:

- 6 graham crackers
- 1 (3½-ounce) good quality milk chocolate or semi-sweet chocolate bar, I like the Israeli or Belgian brands
- 6 marshmallows

Even the youngest cooks among us can whip up these s'mores which would make any Girl Scout envious. There is still something about toasting the marshmallows on sticks around a campfire, but when you are in your kitchen, not the forest, give these a try.

1. Snap the graham crackers on the dotted lines to make 12 (2½ inch) squares. Place 6 of the graham crackers onto a paper or microwave-safe plate. If the plate is too small to hold all 6, divide them among two plates.

2. Unwrap the chocolate bar. Most brands have the chocolate scored into smaller squares. Use these lines to break off squares a little smaller than the graham cracker. Lay the chocolate onto the 6 graham crackers on the plate.

3. Top each one with a marshmallow.

4. Microwave the s'mores for 30 seconds. The marshmallows will be big and puffy.

5. Carefully remove the plate from the oven and quickly top each s'more with a graham cracker.

Makes: 6 s'mores

Hot Pretzels 2 Ways

Equipment list:

- 2 cookie sheets
- parchment paper
- measuring cups and spoons
- large mixing bowl
- knife
- 8-inch square or round baking pan
- spoon
- small mixing bowl
- whisk
- microwave-safe bowl
- pastry brush
- microwave

Ingredient list:

- 2 packets rapid rise yeast
- 2 tablespoons sugar
- 1½ cups warm water
- 3½ cups bread flour or all-purpose flour
- 1 teaspoon salt
- 2 cups hot water
- 1 tablespoon baking powder
- 1 large egg

You can make the traditional salted hot pretzels or, for a sweet version, make the cinnamon-sugar type. Better yet, make one batch of dough and salt half of them and sweeten the other half. The best of both worlds!

1. Preheat the oven to 425° F. Line 2 cookie sheets with parchment paper. Set aside.

2. Place the yeast and sugar into a large mixing bowl. Add the 1½ cups warm water. Stir to dissolve the yeast. Let stand for 7 minutes. Check to see if bubbles are forming. This shows you that the yeast is alive. If there are no bubbles, wait another 3 minutes. If there are still no bubbles, you need to start again with new packets of yeast.

3. Add the flour and salt to the yeast mixture. With your hands, mix the ingredients in the bowl to get them to form a rough dough; it will not be smooth. Transfer the dough to your work surface. This could be a kitchen counter or a piece of parchment paper on a table. Knead the dough. Really push and pull it to get the dough smooth.

4. With a knife, cut the dough into 8 equal pieces. Roll each piece into a long, thin rope, about 12-16 inches long. Twist into a pretzel or any shape that you like.

5. Pour the 2 cups of hot water into the baking pan. Use a spoon to stir in the baking powder. Dip each pretzel, one at a time, into the baking powder solution. Turn each one over and dip the other side.

6. Place the dipped pretzels on the parchment-lined cookie sheets.

For salted pretzels:

1. Place the egg into a small mixing bowl. Beat it with a whisk.

2. Brush the egg onto the pretzels.

3. Sprinkle the pretzels very lightly with kosher salt.

4. Place into the hot oven and bake for 12-15 minutes, until golden brown.

5. Carefully remove the pretzels from the oven and allow them to cool for a few minutes.

For cinnamon sugar pretzels:

1. Place 4 tablespoons of butter into a microwave-safe bowl. Add 2 tablespoons sugar and 1 teaspoon cinnamon. Microwave for 45 seconds to melt the butter. Stir with a spoon. Brush the butter mixture onto the pretzels, saving the extra butter mixture.

2. Place into the hot oven and bake for 12-15 minutes, until golden brown. Carefully remove the pretzels from the oven and brush on more of the butter mixture.

Makes: 8 pretzels

Half Sour Pickles

Parve

Equipment list:

- measuring cups and spoons
- ½ gallon plastic container with lid
- fork
- garlic press

Ingredient list:

- ¾ cup white vinegar
- ⅓ cup kosher salt
- 4 garlic cloves
- 2 sprigs fresh dill
- 2 tablespoons pickling spice
- 6 kirby cucumbers
- water

What kid doesn't like pickles? Now you can make them at home. This recipe takes patience; the cucumbers need at least 10 days to sit in the brine to turn them into pickles. My kids love putting them on skewers and serving pickles on a stick.

1. Pour the vinegar and salt into the container. Mix with a fork.

2. With a garlic press, mince the garlic into the container.

3. Add the whole sprigs of dill and the pickling spices.

4. Place the whole, unpeeled cucumbers into this pickling liquid.

5. Add water to cover the pickles.

6. Cover the container and place into the refrigerator for 10-12 days. The pickles can keep in the refrigerator for three weeks.

Makes: 6 pickles

Meat Mains

Juicy Hamburgers

Equipment list:

- medium mixing bowl
- small bowl
- whisk
- measuring cups and spoons
- garlic press
- latex gloves (optional)
- medium frying pan
- metal spatula
- pastry brush

Ingredient list:

- 1 pound ground beef
- 1 large egg
- ½ cup flavored bread crumbs
- 2 tablespoons soymilk
- 1 tablespoon parve Worcestershire sauce
- 2 garlic cloves
- 2 tablespoons canola oil
- 4 tablespoons favorite bottled barbecue sauce
- hamburger buns

Makes: 4-6 hamburgers

You can be the king or queen of the grill or frying pan with these great hamburgers. Serve them on buns with shredded lettuce, tomatoes, and pickles.

1. Place the ground beef into a medium bowl.

2. Crack the egg into a small bowl and mix with a whisk. Add it to the beef. Add in the bread crumbs, soymilk, and Worcestershire sauce.

3. With your garlic press, mince the 2 cloves of garlic into the meat mixture.

4. If you have latex gloves, it would be a good idea to put them on. With your hands, lightly knead everything in the bowl. Don't over-mix, just make sure all of the ingredients are mixed in. Form the mixture into 4-6 hamburger patties; don't squish them, you want them to stay juicy. Set aside. If you wore gloves, throw them out. If not, wash your hands with warm soapy water.

5. Place the canola oil into a medium frying pan. Heat over medium-low. When the oil is hot, add the hamburger patties. Cook for 5 minutes. After they have cooked for 3 minutes, use a pastry brush to brush them with the barbecue sauce. Make sure they are not burning; if they are, lower the flame.

6. With a spatula, flip the hamburgers over and cook for 5 minutes on the other side. Brush the barbecue sauce on top.

7. Place each hamburger into a bun.

A note about Worcestershire sauce

   All Worcestershire sauce contains anchovies. It the kosher certification marks stands alone, then the percentage of anchovies is less than 1.6% of the whole product. Many rabbinical authorites say that this is okay to use with meat.

   If the kosher certification on the label has a fish notation next to it, the level exceeds 1.6% and you should refrain from using it in meat dishes.

Steak Fajitas

Equipment list:

- cutting board
- sharp knife
- measuring spoons
- large (12-14 inch) frying pan
- wooden spoon or silicone spatula
- garlic press
- medium pot with lid
- plate or paper towel
- microwave

Ingredient list:

- 1 large yellow onion
- 2 tablespoons canola oil
- ½ red bell pepper, washed and dried
- ½ green bell pepper, washed and dried
- 3 cloves garlic
- 1 (1.25 ounce) packet taco or fajita seasoning mix
- ½ pound London broil or filet split
- 1 cup minute rice, the kind that cooks in 5-minutes
- 4 (10-inch) flour tortillas

1. On your cutting board, with a very sharp knife, cut the onion in half and then slice into very thin semi-circles.

2. Place the oil into the frying pan. Turn the heat to medium. When the oil is hot, add the onion. Let the onion cook for 10 minutes, stirring it with your wooden spoon or silicone spatula. If it starts to brown, lower the heat. You want the onion to get golden and caramel-colored.

3. On your cutting board, with a very sharp knife, cut the red and green peppers in half. Throw out the seeds and stem. Cut away any white part from the inside. Slice the peppers into very thin strips. Add them to the frying pan.

4. With your garlic press, mince the garlic right into the pan.

5. Add 2 teaspoons of the taco or fajita seasoning packet. Save the rest, you will need some for the rice. Mix with a wooden spoon to get it into the vegetables.

6. On your cutting board, with a very sharp knife, slice the steak into very thin strips.

7. Add the meat to the pan. It will stick to the pan for a few minutes but it will release when it is ready, usually in 4-5 minutes.

8. Once the meat releases, use your wooden spoon or silicone spatula to toss the meat with the vegetables. Cook for another 5 minutes, stirring often.

9. While the meat is cooking, prepare the rice according to the directions on the box, except that

when you pour the water into the pot, add 2 teaspoons of the taco or fajita seasoning packet to the water. The rice will soak up these spices as it cooks.

10. Place the tortillas on a plate or paper towel. Warm the tortilla in the microwave oven for 15 seconds.

11. When the rice and steak are done, spoon some of the steak and vegetables and some of the rice into the center of each flour tortilla. Fold each fajita in half, like a taco.

Makes: 4 fajitas

Sloppy Joes

Equipment list:

- large (12-14 inch) frying pan
- wooden spoon or silicone spatula
- can opener
- measuring spoons
- cutting board
- sharp knife

Ingredient list:

- 1 tablespoon canola oil
- 1 pound ground beef
- 1 (28-ounce) can tomato purée
- 1 tablespoon parve Worcestershire sauce
- 1 teaspoon salt
- ½ teaspoon onion powder
- ½ teaspoon garlic powder
- 1 teaspoon dried minced onion
- ¼ teaspoon chili powder
- 1 tablespoon apple cider vinegar
- 1 tablespoon light corn syrup
- 1 tablespoon dark brown sugar
- ½ small green bell pepper
- hamburger buns

1. Place the canola oil into a large frying pan.

2. Turn the heat to medium.

3. When the oil is hot, add the ground beef. Poke it with the wooden spoon or silicone spatula to break up the chunks and stir often to brown all the pieces.

4. Use your can opener and open the can of tomato purée.

5. When the meat is no longer pink, add the tomato purée to the pan. Add the Worcestershire sauce, salt, onion powder, garlic powder, dried minced onion, chili powder, apple cider vinegar, light corn syrup, and brown sugar. Use your wooden spoon to combine.

6. On your cutting board, with a sharp knife, cut the ½ green pepper into long thin strips. Chop those strips into tiny little pieces and add them to the pan.

7. Allow the mixture to cook for 5-6 minutes, mixing it from time to time.

8. Serve the Sloppy Joe mixture on hamburger buns.

A note about Worcestershire sauce
  All Worcestershire sauce contains anchovies. It the kosher certification marks stands alone, then the percentage of anchovies is less than 1.6% of the whole product. Many rabbinical authorites say that this is okay to use with meat.
  If the kosher certification on the label has a fish notation next to it, the level exceeds 1.6% and you should refrain from using it in meat dishes.

Makes: 4-6 sloppy joes

Deli Faces

Equipment list:

- medium pot
- strainer
- cookie sheet
- parchment paper
- 4 salad plates
- very small round cookie cutters
- scissors
- toothpick

Ingredient list:

- 1 teaspoon salt
- 4 ounces spaghetti or rotini pasta
- ketchup or jarred marinara sauce
- 8 chicken nuggets
- 4 pieces of turkey roll
- 2 pieces of salami

Makes: 4 faces

Ask any kid to list their favorite foods and salami, pasta and chicken nuggets are bound to make the short list. This dish uses them all in a fun presentation that is sure to be a crowd pleaser. You could swap out the chicken nuggets for mini hot dogs or think up your own twist.

1. Preheat the oven to 375° F.

2. Fill a pot ¾ths of the way with water. Add salt to the water. Place the pot over medium heat and bring the water to a boil. Add the pasta and cook it for as many minutes as the package says to, until it is al denté (slightly chewy, not mushy).

3. When it is done, place the strainer into the sink and pour the pasta into it to drain the water. You can mix the pasta with ketchup or marinara sauce, or leave it plain.

4. While the pasta is cooking, prepare the chicken nuggets. Place the frozen nuggets onto a cookie sheet that is lined with parchment paper. Bake for 15 minutes, or until they are cooked.

5. While the pasta is cooking and the chicken nuggets are baking, you can set up the face. Lay a piece of turkey roll in the center of the salad plate. Using the small round cookie cutters and scissors, cut out 2 salami circles for eyes and a smile shape for the mouth. Do this for each of the 4 turkey roll faces.

6. Using a toothpick, add ketchup eyeballs and a nose.

7. Arrange the cooked pasta for hair. Add the baked chicken nuggets as ears.

Chicken Pot Pie

Equipment list:

- kitchen towel
- cutting board
- sharp knife
- large pot
- measuring cups and spoons
- spoon or silicone spatula
- 4 oven-safe ramekins (4-5 inch diameter)
- ladle
- rolling pin
- small cookie cutters
- cookie sheet

Ingredient list:

- ½ (17.5 ounce) box puff pastry
- 1 small onion
- 2 tablespoons canola oil
- 2 tablespoons margarine
- 2 stalks celery
- 1 (10-ounce) box frozen vegetables, mix of peas and carrots
- 3 tablespoons all-purpose flour
- 1 cup chicken stock
- ¼ cup soy milk
- 2 boneless, skinless chicken breasts (cutlets)
- salt and black pepper

1. Preheat the oven to 400° F.

2. Remove the puff pastry from the freezer. Take 1 sheet out of the package and return the second sheet to the freezer. Lightly cover the puff pastry sheet with a kitchen towel and allow it to thaw for 20 minutes as you prepare the pot pie filling.

3. On your cutting board, with a sharp knife, chop the onion into small pieces.

4. Place the oil into a large pot over medium heat. When the oil is hot, add the margarine and let it melt. Carefully add the chopped onion and cook for 5-6 minutes, making sure the onions don't burn. If they start to brown, lower the heat.

5. While the onions are cooking, slice each celery stalk into 3-4 long strips and then chop into small pieces. Carefully add the celery, peas, and carrots to the pot. Cook for 4-5 minutes.

6. Sprinkle in the flour. Mix with a spoon or silicone spatula, it will be sticky. Add in the chicken stock and soy milk. Cook until the mixture is thickened, about 5 minutes.

7. On your cutting board, with a sharp knife, cut the chicken into cubes, the size of board game dice. Add the cubes of chicken to the pot, season with salt and black pepper, and then remove the pot from the heat.

8. Ladle the pot pie mixture into 4 individual oven-safe ramekins.

9. Cut the puff pastry sheet into 4 (4-inch) squares.

With your rolling pin, roll each square to form a 6-inch square. Save the extra dough.

10. Cover each ramekin with a square of puff pastry, tucking the pastry over the edge to keep it secured. Use a small cookie cutter to make decorations out of the leftover puff pastry and place on top of each pot pie.

11. Place the ramekins on a cookie sheet and place the cookie sheet into the preheated oven.

12. Bake for 25 minutes, until the pastry is golden brown and the filling is bubbly.

Makes: 4 pot pies

Zesty Chicken

Equipment list:

- 8-inch square baking dish
- small mixing bowl
- measuring cups and spoons
- spoon

Ingredient list:

- 5 pieces of chicken, with bone and skin, you can use the legs, thighs or the breast
- ¼ cup mayonnaise
- 2 tablespoons ketchup
- 2 teaspoons dry onion soup mix

Remember to carefully wash your hands and anything that came in contact with the raw chicken.

1. Preheat oven to 350° F.

2. Wash and dry the chicken pieces and place them into the square baking dish.

3. In a small mixing bowl, mix the mayonnaise, ketchup, and onion soup mix. Stir with a spoon to combine.

4. Pour the dressing mixture over the chicken and spread it over each piece.

5. Place the baking dish into the hot oven and bake uncovered, for 1 hour or until the chicken is done.

Makes: 5 pieces

Shake and Bake Chicken

Meat

E quipment list:

⁶ shallow bowl

⁶ fork

⁶ gallon size heavy duty Ziploc® bag

⁶ 8-inch square baking dish

I ngredient list:

⁶ 1 large egg

⁶ ½ cup corn flake crumbs

⁶ 5 pieces of chicken, with bone and skin, you can use the legs, thighs or the breast

⁶ honey

I love putting on some music and shaking the bag around as I coat my chicken. You can add in fresh herbs like oregano or chopped basil to the bag of crumbs before shaking in the chicken. Feel free to double or triple this recipe. Once your family tastes it you will need to!

Remember to carefully wash your hands and anything that came in contact with the raw chicken.

1. Preheat oven to 350° F.

2. Crack the egg into a shallow bowl. Beat the egg with a fork.

3. Pour the corn flake crumbs into a Ziploc® bag.

4. Wash and dry the chicken pieces.

5. Take a piece of the chicken and dip it into the egg, turning to coat it on all sides.

6. Drop the coated piece into the Ziploc® bag. Close the bag and shake to coat the chicken well with the corn flake crumbs.

7. Remove the piece of coated chicken and place it into the baking dish.

8. Repeat the steps until all five pieces are coated and in the dish.

9. Drizzle the top of each piece of chicken with honey.

10. Place into the hot oven uncovered and bake for 1 hour or until the chicken is done.

M akes: 5 pieces

Easy Meat Roast

Meat

Equipment list:

- heavy baking pan
- cutting board
- sharp knife
- garlic press
- measuring cups and spoons
- small mixing bowl
- aluminum foil

Ingredient list:

- 4 pound California roast, beef brisket, or shell roast
- 1 large onion
- 5 garlic cloves, minced
- ½ cup ketchup
- ½ cup chili sauce
- 3 tablespoons brown sugar

You can lend a hand and impress your family and cook the main dish for a Shabbos or holiday meal. This roast is so easy and so delicious. You are sure to win rave reviews.

1. Preheat oven to 350° F.

2. Place the meat into a heavy baking pan that is just big enough to hold it.

3. On your cutting board, with a sharp knife, slice the onion into rings. Spread the onions over the meat.

4. Place the cloves of garlic, one at a time, into your garlic press. Squeeze the press so that the minced garlic gets all over the meat.

5. Pour the ketchup, chili sauce, and brown sugar into a small bowl. Stir to mix. Pour over the meat.

6. Cover the pan with aluminum foil and place into the hot oven for 2½ hours.

7. When the meat is done, carefully remove it from the oven. When it is cool enough to handle, carefully slice it into thin slices. You can re-heat it in the sauce.

Makes: 8-10 servings

Beef and Broccoli Lo Mein

Equipment list:

- large pot
- strainer
- measuring spoons
- tongs
- cutting board
- sharp knife
- large frying pan
- garlic press
- small mixing bowl

Ingredient list:

- 8 ounces (½ box) angel hair pasta or thin spaghetti
- 3 tablespoons soy sauce
- 2 tablespoons roasted or toasted sesame oil
- 2 tablespoons sugar
- ½ large onion
- 3 cups chopped broccoli
- 1 tablespoon canola oil
- 4 garlic cloves
- 1 teaspoon ground ginger
- 1 pound London broil or filet split
- 1 teaspoon beef bouillon powder
- ½ cup water
- 3 tablespoons soy sauce
- 1 tablespoons hoisin sauce

Who needs take-out when you can make something this delicious?

1. Fill a large pot ¾ths of the way with water. Bring the pot of water to a boil over high heat.

2. When the water boils, add the pasta and cook it for as many minutes as the package says to until it is al denté (slightly chewy, not mushy).

3. Remove 1 strand of pasta and taste to make sure it is done. If it is, pour the pasta into a strainer over the sink. Drain out the water and dump the pasta back into your pot.

4. Add the 3 tablespoons of soy sauce, sesame oil, and sugar to the pasta. Toss with tongs to coat all of the pieces well. Set aside.

5. On your cutting board, with a sharp knife, slice the onion half into thin slices. If your broccoli florets are big, chop them into bite sized pieces with the knife as well.

6. Place the canola oil into a large frying pan. Heat over medium. When the oil is hot, add the onions and broccoli to the pan. Sauté for 4 minutes.

7. With a garlic press, mince the garlic right into the pan. Add the ginger.

8. On your cutting board, with a sharp knife, slice the meat as thinly as you can into strips. Add the meat to the pan and sauté for 5 minutes; the meat should no longer be red.

9. In a small bowl, mix the beef bouillon powder and

the water. Add the 3 tablespoons soy sauce and hoisin sauce. Mix until combined. Add this sauce to the meat and broccoli.

10. Add the pasta into the pan and with your tongs mix it all together.

11. Transfer to plates or a serving bowl.

Makes: 6 servings

Dairy Mains

Spaghetti With 3 Tomato Sauce

Parve

Equipment list:

- cutting board
- sharp knife
- measuring spoons
- 2 large pots, one with lid
- can opener
- wooden spoon
- fork
- strainer

Ingredient list:

- 1 medium onion
- 4 garlic cloves, peeled
- 3 tablespoons extra virgin olive oil
- 1 (28-ounce) can crushed tomatoes
- 1 (14.5-ounce) can diced tomatoes
- ¼ teaspoon crushed red pepper flakes
- ¼ teaspoon salt
- ¼ teaspoon freshly ground black pepper
- 13-15 fresh cherry tomatoes
- 16 ounces spaghetti (usually 1 box), uncooked

1. On your cutting board, with a sharp knife, chop the onion into small dice. Cut the garlic cloves into small chunks and set the onions and garlic aside.

2. Pour the oil into one of the pots and heat over medium-low for 2 minutes. Add the chopped onion and garlic to the hot oil. Cook for 6-7 minutes, stirring from time to time with a wooden spoon. Make sure the onions are not turning brown; if they are, lower the heat.

3. Meanwhile, using your can opener, open the cans of crushed tomatoes and diced tomatoes. Carefully pour them into the pot. Add the crushed red pepper flakes, salt, and black pepper. Cover the pot and cook for 15 minutes.

4. Rinse and dry the cherry tomatoes. On your cutting board, with a sharp knife, slice each cherry tomato in half.

5. After the sauce has cooked for 15 minutes, add the cherry tomatoes. Cover the pot and cook for 15 minutes longer.

6. While the sauce is cooking, fill a large pot ¾ths of the way with water. Add 1 tablespoon of salt to the water and place the pot on the stove. Bring the pot of salted water to a boil over high heat.

7. When the water boils, add the spaghetti and cook it for as many minutes as the package says to until it is al denté (slightly chewy, not mushy).

8. Carefully remove 1 strand of spaghetti with a fork and taste to make sure it is done. If it is, pour the spaghetti into a strainer over the sink. Drain out the water. Empty the spaghetti into a big serving bowl.

9. Ladle the sauce over the spaghetti and toss to coat.

Makes: 8 servings

Sweet Cheese Toasts

quipment list:

⁶ toaster oven

⁶ aluminum foil

⁶ small mixing bowl

⁶ measuring cups and spoons

⁶ spoon

⁶ knife

Ingredient list:

⁶ 2 slices white or whole wheat bread

⁶ ½ cup cottage cheese

⁶ ½ teaspoon cinnamon

⁶ 3 teaspoons sugar

This was the very first recipe that my Mom taught me when I was a kid. I loved it then and still love it now.

1. Place 2 slices of bread in the toaster oven and toast lightly. Remove from the toaster and set aside on a piece of aluminum foil.

2. Place the cottage cheese into a small mixing bowl. Add the cinnamon and sugar. With your spoon, mix to combine the ingredients.

3. Spoon out half of the cottage cheese mixture onto one slice of bread and the other half onto the second slice of bread.

4. Place the foil into the toaster oven and toast for 1 cycle on medium heat.

5. With your knife, carefully cut each piece of bread into small squares or triangles.

akes: 2 servings

Tuna Melts

Equipment list:

- aluminum foil
- can opener
- small mixing bowl
- fork
- cutting board
- sharp knife
- measuring spoon

Ingredient list:

- 1 English muffin or 2 slices of rye bread
- 1 (6-ounce can) white tuna
- ½ stalk celery
- ¼ of a small red onion, optional
- 3 tablespoons of mayonnaise
- freshly ground black pepper
- ½ tomato, optional
- 2 slices of American or Cheddar cheese

You can make this dish in the toaster oven or in the regular oven set to broil.

1. Spread open the English muffin and lay it flat on a piece of aluminum foil. If you are using rye bread, place the two pieces on the aluminum foil. Place in the toaster oven and toast on medium to get the bread lightly brown so it will not get soggy from the tuna fish. You can also place the bread into the oven set to broil and broil the bread for 3 minutes.

2. With your can opener, open the can of tuna fish. Press the top of the can into the tuna then turn over to drain out the liquid. Empty the fish into a small mixing bowl. With a fork, break up the chunks of tuna.

3. Rinse and dry the celery stalks. On your cutting board, with a sharp knife, trim off the root of the celery. Chop the celery into tiny pieces. Measure 1 tablespoon and add it to the tuna. Reserve the rest for another use.

4. If you are using the onion, on your cutting board, with a sharp knife, chop your ¼ onion into tiny pieces. Measure 1 tablespoon and add to the tuna. Reserve the rest for another use.

5. Add the mayonnaise to the tuna. Mix it all together with the fork. Add a pinch of black pepper, or 3-4 turns of a peppermill to taste.

6. Carefully remove the bread from the toaster or broiler.

7. Divide the tuna and place a mound on each piece of English muffin or bread.

8. If you are using the tomato, place it on your cutting board and with a sharp knife slice off two very thin slices. Place a slice on top of each tuna mound.

9. Top with a piece of cheese.

10. Return the tuna melts to the toaster and toast until the cheese is melted. If you are using an oven, return the tuna melts to the oven and broil for 3 minutes until the cheese is melted.

Makes: 2 tuna melts

Pizza Bubble Ring

Equipment list:

- 10-inch tube pan
- microwave-safe bowl or small pot
- microwave
- garlic press
- measuring cups and spoons
- spoon
- sharp knife
- small pot

Ingredient list:

- nonstick cooking spray, like Pam®
- 8 tablespoons (1 stick) butter
- 2 garlic cloves
- 1 teaspoon oregano
- ½ teaspoon garlic powder
- ½ teaspoon onion powder
- ½ teaspoon freshly ground black pepper
- ¼ teaspoon crushed red pepper flakes
- 2 pounds fresh or frozen pizza dough, thawed
- 8 ounces shredded mozzarella cheese
- 2 tablespoons Parmesan cheese
- 1½ cups pizza sauce from a jar

What kid doesn't like pizza? Here is a funky spin on the traditional. Even the youngest chefs can help out on this one. My local Pathmark supermarket carries frozen pizza dough which I always keep in my freezer. I just defrost it for a few hours and then begin my recipe. The local pizza store will also sell you pizza dough by the pound, or you can make your own.

1. Preheat the oven to 350° F.

2. Spray the tube pan with nonstick cooking spray. Make sure to spray the tube as well. Set aside.

3. Place the butter into a microwave-safe bowl. Place in the microwave for 1 minute to melt. You can also do this in a small pot over low heat.

4. With your garlic press, mince the 2 cloves of garlic into the butter. Add the oregano, garlic powder, onion powder, black pepper, and crushed red pepper flakes. Stir with a spoon to combine.

5. With a sharp knife, carefully divide the dough into 40 small balls.

6. Flatten one of the balls and place some of the mozzarella into the center of it. Roll the dough up around the cheese to enclose it. Do this with all 40 balls.

7. Dip each ball into the butter/spice mixture and place into the prepared tube pan.

8. Sprinkle the Parmesan over the dough balls. Drizzle on any extra butter mixture.

9. Place into the oven and bake for 35 minutes or until golden brown.

10. Let cool for 5 minutes then carefully lift the tube from the sides of the pan.

11. Place the tube on a serving plate.

12. Warm the pizza sauce in a small pot over medium heat. Serve the pizza bubble ring warm with the pizza sauce.

Makes: 8 servings

Mac and Cheese

Dairy

Equipment list:

- large pot
- strainer
- silicone spatula or wooden spoon
- measuring cups and spoons

Ingredient list:

- 2 teaspoons salt
- 2 cups elbow macaroni, uncooked
- 1 tablespoon butter
- 2 slices yellow American cheese
- 1 cup shredded Cheddar cheese
- ½ cup whole milk or 2% milk

While the orange stuff that comes in a box is alright every once in a while, it is great to know how to make your own creamy mac and cheese. This recipe could not be easier.

1. Fill the large pot ¾ths of the way with water. Add the salt.

2. Bring the pot of salted water to a boil over high heat.

3. When the water boils, add the macaroni and cook it for as many minutes as the package says to until it is al denté (slightly chewy, not mushy).

4. Carefully remove 1 piece of macaroni to taste to make sure it is done. If it is, pour the macaroni into a strainer over the sink.

5. Meanwhile, while the macaroni is draining, prepare the cheese sauce in the macaroni pot.

6. Place the butter, American cheese, Cheddar cheese, and milk into the pot. Heat over medium-low, mixing with a silicone spatula or wooden spoon until melted and creamy.

7. Add the cooked macaroni to the pot and toss to coat with the cheese sauce.

8. Scoop into a serving plate or bowl.

Makes: 4 servings

Bean, Rice, and Cheese Burritos

Dairy

Equipment list:

- measuring cups and spoons
- medium pot with lid
- fork
- can opener
- aluminum foil

Ingredient list:

- 1 cup water
- 1 tablespoon fajita seasoning spice, from a 1.25-ounce packet, like Ortega® brand
- 1 cup instant white rice, the kind that is ready in 5 minutes, like Minute Rice®
- 4 large flour tortillas
- 2 cups shredded Cheddar cheese
- 8 tablespoons refried kidney or pinto beans (from a 15-ounce can)
- sour cream
- jarred salsa

Makes: 4 burritos

This recipe is a great introduction to the world of burritos. You can sauté some onions and peppers with some of the spice from the fajita seasoning packet and add them to the burrito. I always serve mine with tortilla chips. You can make them in advance and keep them wrapped in the refrigerator and then heat them in a hot oven.

1. Preheat oven to 400° F.

2. Place the water and fajita seasoning spice into a medium pot. Over medium heat, bring the water to a boil.

3. Stir in the rice. Cover the pot and remove it from the heat. Let the rice stand for 5 minutes. Fluff with a fork. Set aside.

4. Lay the 4 tortillas on a work surface in front of you. Scoop ¼ cup of the cooked rice into the center of each tortilla. Add ½ cup of the shredded Cheddar cheese to each.

5. With your can opener, open the can of refried beans. Spoon 2 tablespoons of the refried beans onto the rice and cheese.

6. Roll in the sides of 1 tortilla and then roll it up, tucking the filling in as you roll to make your burrito. Do this with the other 3 tortillas.

7. Wrap each burrito in aluminum foil. Place the wrapped burritos into the oven and bake for 15 minutes to melt the cheese and warm the beans.

8. Serve with sour cream and salsa.

Side Dishes

Carrot Muffins

Parve

Equipment list:

- measuring cups and spoons
- medium mixing bowl
- small silicone spatula or spoon
- electric mixer
- paper muffin cups
- cupcake or muffin tray
- toothpick

Ingredient list:

- 1 cup sugar
- 1 cup all-purpose flour
- ¾ cup canola oil
- 12 ounces baby food carrots (usually 3 jars)
- 1 teaspoon baking soda
- 1 teaspoon cinnamon
- 2 large eggs

My mom used to make these all the time when I was growing up. They were always a hit with me and my friends.

1. Preheat the oven to 350° F.

2. Place the sugar, flour, and oil into a medium mixing bowl. Add the baby food carrots, using your small spatula or a spoon to get all of the baby food out of the jar.

3. Add the baking soda, cinnamon, and eggs.

4. Mix with an electric mixer at medium speed for 3 minutes, until the batter is smooth.

5. Place the paper muffin cups into a muffin or cupcake tray.

6. If your measuring cup has a spout, pour the batter from the measuring cup into the muffin cups; if not, use a large spoon. Fill the muffin cups almost to the top.

7. Place tray into the oven and bake for 30 minutes.

8. Open the oven and carefully pull out the muffin tray. Stick a toothpick into the center of a muffin; it should come out clean. If is comes out gooey, return the muffins to the oven for another 2-3 minutes. When the muffins are done, remove from the oven and allow the muffins to cool.

Makes: 12-14 muffins

Noodle Rice

Equipment list:

- measuring cups and spoons
- medium frying pan
- wooden spoon or silicone spatula
- small mixing bowl
- spoon
- 8-inch round or square ceramic or glass baking dish
- knife
- aluminum foil

Ingredient list:

- 2 tablespoons margarine
- 4 ounces (usually ¼ box) of angel hair, thin spaghetti, or capellini pasta, uncooked
- 2 teaspoons dried minced onion
- 1 teaspoon beef bouillon powder (meat or parve)
- 1 teaspoon onion powder
- ⅛ teaspoon celery salt
- 1 cup long grain enriched rice (not 5 minute or boil in bag type), uncooked
- 2 cups chicken stock or vegetable stock
- 3 tablespoons margarine

This side dish goes with so many things and you can add in your own ingredients. Try sliced mushrooms or broccoli florets chopped up very small. Use your imagination to change it every time you make it until you find your favorite.

1. Place the margarine into the frying pan. Turn the heat to medium and melt the margarine.

2. Break the pasta into 1-inch pieces and add them to the frying pan. Fry until the pasta turns light brown, mixing with a wooden spoon or silicone spatula to make sure none of the pasta is sticking or burning.

3. Preheat the oven to 350° F.

4. In a small bowl, combine the minced onion, beef bouillon powder, onion powder, and celery salt. Stir with a spoon to mix together. Set aside.

5. Place the rice into the baking dish. Add in the browned pasta, chicken stock and the spice mixture. Mix it all together.

6. Use a knife to cut the margarine into 8 cubes. Scatter the margarine cubes over the top of the rice.

7. Cover the dish tightly with aluminum foil. Carefully place into the oven and bake for 1 hour.

Makes: 8 servings

Un-fried Spicy Fries

Parve

Equipment list:

- cookie sheet
- parchment paper
- measuring cups and spoons
- cutting board
- sharp knife
- 2 shallow bowls
- whisk
- fork

Ingredient list:

- 3 tablespoons canola oil
- 3 medium Russet potatoes
- ¾ cup all-purpose flour
- 1 teaspoon garlic powder
- 1 teaspoon onion powder
- 1 teaspoon salt
- ½-1 teaspoon freshly ground black pepper (20-40 turns of a pepper mill depending on how spicy you want them)
- 2 teaspoons paprika
- ¼ teaspoon chili powder
- ¼ teaspoon celery salt
- 2 large eggs
- nonstick cooking spray, like Pam®

A spicy, healthier version of the french fry. They look great and taste delicious.

1. Preheat the oven to 450° F.

2. Line the cookie sheet with parchment paper.

3. Spoon the canola oil onto the parchment paper and tilt the cookie sheet to get an even coating of oil. Set aside.

4. On your cutting board, with a sharp knife, cut each potato in half lengthwise. Cut each half into 4 equal wedges. Set aside.

5. Place the flour into one of the shallow bowls. Add the garlic powder, onion powder, salt, black pepper, paprika, chili powder, and celery salt. Mix with a whisk or a fork to evenly combine the spices with the flour.

6. Crack the eggs into the second shallow bowl and whisk them until light and fluffy.

7. Use a fork to dip each potato wedge into the egg, making sure both sides are coated. Immediately place this coated potato wedge into the flour mixture. Shake the bowl around to completely coat the wedge. Try not to use your fingers or the coating will come off. Use a fork to transfer the potato wedge to the prepared baking sheet. Do this with all of the potato wedges.

8. When all of the wedges are coated in the batter and placed on the baking sheet, spray them with the nonstick cooking spray.

9. Place the sheet into the hot oven and bake for 20 minutes.

10. Open the oven and carefully remove the tray. With a fork, flip each wedge over. Place the tray back into the oven and bake for another 15 minutes.

Makes: 6 servings

Sesame Broccoli

Parve

Equipment list:

- large pot with lid
- measuring cups and spoons
- wooden spoon or silicone spatula
- strainer

Ingredient list:

- 12 ounces broccoli florets
- 1 cup water
- 1 tablespoon roasted or toasted sesame oil
- ¼ cup soy sauce
- 2 tablespoons honey
- 1 tablespoon sesame seeds

This recipe works great with green beans too.

1. Place the broccoli florets into a large pot. Add the water.

2. Bring the water to a boil over medium heat. Cover the pot and let the broccoli steam for 7-8 minutes.

3. Remove the lid. The broccoli should be bright green and softened. Mix the broccoli with a wooden spoon or silicone spatula.

4. Place a strainer into the sink and carefully drain any water out of the broccoli.

5. Return the broccoli to the pot. Add the sesame oil, soy sauce, honey and sesame seeds. Mix to combine. Turn the heat to medium and cook for 3-4 minutes.

6. Remove from the heat and serve.

Makes: 4-6 servings

Peach Noodle Kugel

Parve

Equipment list:

- 8-inch square baking pan
- large pot
- measuring cups and spoons
- large mixing bowl
- whisk or electric mixer
- can opener
- strainer
- cutting board
- sharp knife
- silicone spatula or wooden spoon
- small bowl

Ingredient list:

- nonstick cooking spray
- 8 ounces medium noodles (usually ½ a box)
- 3 large eggs
- ¼ cup orange juice
- ⅓ cup sugar
- ½ teaspoon salt
- ¼ cup apple sauce
- 1 (15¼-ounce) can sliced peaches in syrup
- 4 tablespoons margarine
- 1 teaspoon cinnamon
- 1 tablespoon sugar

Sometimes it is fun to help your family prepare for a Shabbos or holiday meal. This noodle kugel would go great with any meal.

1. Preheat oven to 350° F.

2. Spray an 8-inch square baking pan with nonstick cooking spray. Set aside.

3. Fill a large pot ¾ths of the way with water. Bring the pot of water to a boil over high heat. When the water boils, add the noodles and cook for as many minutes as the package says to until the noodles are al denté (slightly chewy, not mushy).

4. Meanwhile, crack the eggs into a large mixing bowl. Add the orange juice, sugar, salt, and apple sauce. With your whisk or an electric mixer, beat all of the ingredients together.

5. With your can opener, open the can of peaches. Place the strainer over your mixing bowl. Empty the can into the strainer, letting the syrup drip into the batter in the mixing bowl. Mix in the syrup.

6. Place the strained peaches on your cutting board. Set 8 of the peach slices aside. With your knife, chop the rest of the peaches into 1-inch cubes. Set aside.

7. When the noodles are done, place your strainer into the sink. Carefully drain the noodles by pouring them into the strainer and shaking out the water.

8. Immediately place the hot noodles back into the pot and add the margarine. The heat from the noodles will melt the margarine. With a silicone

spatula or wooden spoon, stir to mix the melted margarine into the noodles. Add the egg mixture and the cubed peaches to the pot of noodles. Toss to combine.

9. Pour the noodle mixture into your prepared baking pan.

10. Take the 8 sliced peaches and place them in 2 rows of 4 on top of the kugel.

11. In a small cup or bowl, mix the teaspoon of cinnamon with the tablespoon of sugar. Shake the cup or bowl to combine.

12. With your fingertips, sprinkle the cinnamon/sugar mixture all over the top of the kugel.

13. Place the pan into the hot oven and bake, uncovered, for 45 minutes.

Makes: 9 servings

Breaded Cauliflower

Parve

Equipment list:

- cookie sheet
- parchment paper
- cutting board
- sharp knife
- large mixing bowl
- measuring cups and spoons
- plastic wrap
- small bowl
- fork

Ingredient list:

- 1 head cauliflower
- 2 tablespoons canola oil
- 2 large eggs
- ½ cup corn flake crumbs or bread crumbs

1. Preheat the oven to 350° F.

2. Line the cookie sheet with parchment paper. Set aside.

3. Hold your cauliflower on its side on your cutting board. With a sharp knife, cut off the cauliflower florets into bite sized pieces and place them into a large mixing bowl. Discard the hard center of the cauliflower.

4. Add the oil to the bowl. Cover the bowl tightly with plastic wrap. Shake the bowl to coat the florets.

5. Crack the eggs into a small mixing bowl. Lightly beat them with a fork. Uncover the bowl, add the eggs and re-cover. You may need a fresh piece of plastic wrap to get it to stick. Shake the bowl again to coat the cauliflower with the eggs.

6. Uncover the bowl and add the cornflake crumbs or bread crumbs. Re-cover the bowl and seal with the plastic wrap. Shake to coat the cauliflower.

7. Place the breaded cauliflower onto the prepared cookie sheet in a single layer.

8. Place the cookie sheet into the oven and bake for 35 minutes.

9. When the baking time is done, carefully stick a fork into one of the pieces and make sure it is soft. If it is still hard, return the cauliflower to the oven and bake for another 5-10 minutes. When it is done, remove the cauliflower from the oven and serve.

Makes: 4-6 servings

Stuffed Baked Potatoes

Dairy

Equipment list:

- knife
- baking sheet
- pasty brush
- small bowl
- measuring cups and spoons
- scissors
- small pot
- strainer
- cutting board
- sharp knife
- wooden spoon or silicone spatula

Ingredient list:

- 3 large Russet potatoes
- olive oil

Sour Cream and Chive topping:

- ½ cup sour cream
- 6 chives

Salsa Cheddar topping:

- ¾ cup bottled salsa
- ⅓ cup shredded Cheddar cheese

Broccoli Cheddar topping:

- 1 cup broccoli florets
- ½ cup shredded Cheddar cheese
- 2 teaspoons flour
- 2 teaspoons milk
- ½ teaspoon salt

Any of these filling recipes makes enough to fill three potatoes.

1. Preheat oven to 400° F.

2. Scrub each potato to make sure it is clean. Dry them.

3. With a knife, cut a large deep "x" into the top of each potato. Place the potatoes onto a baking sheet. With a pastry brush, brush olive oil all over each potato. Place into the hot oven and bake for 1 hour. When the potatoes are done, carefully remove them from the oven.

4. With paper towels to protect your fingers, push the ends of the potatoes, to the center to open the slit more fully and help fluff the potatoes.

5. Prepare your topping of choice.

Sour Cream and Chive topping:

1. Place the sour cream into a small bowl.

2. With a pair of scissors, snip the chives into tiny pieces. Add them to the bowl. Stir to combine. Place a large spoonful into the slit of the potato.

Salsa Cheddar topping:

1. Place ¼ cup of the salsa into the slit of each potato, it will leak out of the opening. Top each potato with ⅓ of the Cheddar cheese. Return the potatoes to the oven for 5 minutes, until the cheese is melted.

Broccoli Cheddar topping:

1. Place the broccoli florets on a cutting board and chop them with a sharp knife into ¾ inch pieces.

Place the chopped broccoli into a small pot. Add water to cover. Bring to a boil over medium heat. Cook the broccoli until tender, about 5-6 minutes.

2. Place a strainer into the sink. Empty the broccoli into it and drain out the water. Return the broccoli to the pot. Add the cheese.

3. Place the flour into a small bowl. Add the milk and stir to dissolve. Add this flour mixture to the pot. Add the salt.

4. Heat over medium, stirring with a wooden spoon or silicone spatula until the cheese is melted and smooth. Pour ⅓ into each potato slit; it will overflow down the sides.

Makes: 3 stuffed baked potatoes

Sweet Potato Pie

Equipment list:

- can opener
- strainer
- medium mixing bowl
- fork or potato masher
- measuring cups and spoons
- electric mixer
- cookie sheet

Ingredient list:

- 1 (15.75-ounce) can sweet potatoes or 1 cup mashed from a larger can
- 1 cup soymilk
- ¾ cup dark brown sugar
- ¼ cup all-purpose flour
- 2 large eggs
- 1½ teaspoons ground cinnamon
- ⅛ teaspoon salt
- 1 (9-inch) ready-to-bake pie crust

When I was growing up, this sweet potato pie was always on my mom's holiday table. The pie crusts are usually sold 3 in a package. You can just use the one and return the others to the freezer or you can experiment with the remaining two to make strips of dough and assemble into a lattice design.

1. Preheat the oven to 400° F.

2. With your can opener, open the can of sweet potatoes. Pour into a strainer over the sink to drain out all of the liquid.

3. Place the sweet potatoes into a medium mixing bowl. Mash them with the back of a fork or potato masher.

4. Add the soymilk, brown sugar, flour eggs, cinnamon, and salt.

5. With an electric mixer at medium speed, mix all of the ingredients until the mixture becomes a smooth batter.

6. Place the pie crust on a cookie sheet. Pour the batter into the pie crust.

7. Transfer the cookie sheet into the hot oven and bake the pie for 10 minutes.

8. Turn the oven temperature down to 350° F and bake for another 40 minutes.

9. Carefully remove the sweet potato pie from the oven. Slice and serve.

Makes: 10-12 servings

Drinks

Creamy Rich Hot Chocolate

Dairy

Equipment list:

- knife
- heavy medium pot
- measuring spoons and cups
- whisk or wooden spoon
- ladle
- mugs

Ingredient list:

- 2 cups light cream or half and half
- 2 cups whole milk
- 4 ounces good quality milk chocolate, chopped or broken
- 4 ounces good quality bittersweet or semi-sweet chocolate, chopped or broken into very small pieces
- 1 tablespoon dark corn syrup
- whipped cream or marshmallows, optional

What could be better on a cold, wintery day? Don't reach for the hot water and cocoa powder just yet. Follow this recipe and you will be rewarded with a rich, creamy mug full of intense chocolate flavor. Break or chop the chocolate fairly small so that it will melt quickly. If you don't have light cream or half and half in the house, you could use whole milk instead.

1. Place the light cream or half and half into a heavy medium pot. Add the milk, chopped milk chocolate, and the bittersweet or semi-sweet chocolate. Stir in the corn syrup with your whisk or wooden spoon.

2. Cook over low heat until the chocolate is melted and the mixture is smooth. Continue to stir as it cooks. Make sure the heat stays low so the chocolate doesn't burn.

3. To serve, ladle the hot chocolate into mugs. Top with whipped cream or marshmallows, if desired.

Makes: 6 (6 ounce) servings

White Hot Chocolate

Dairy

Equipment list:

- measuring spoons and cups
- heavy medium pot
- whisk or wooden spoon
- ladle
- mugs
- vegetable peeler

Ingredient list:

- 1 cup heavy cream
- 2 cups whole milk
- 2 tablespoons sugar
- 1 teaspoon pure vanilla extract
- 4 ounces good quality white chocolate
- whipped cream, optional
- extra white chocolate and milk chocolate for shaving

Comfy, cozy, warm and white. Make sure you use good quality white chocolate, not baking bars, but good chocolate bars that you would want to eat.

1. Place the heavy cream into a heavy medium pot. Add the milk and sugar. Stir in the vanilla. Break the white chocolate into small pieces and add them to the pot.

2. Cook over low heat until the chocolate is melted and the mixture is smooth. Use a whisk or wooden spoon to stir as it cooks. Make sure the heat stays low so the chocolate doesn't burn.

3. To serve, ladle the white hot chocolate into mugs. Top with whipped cream, if desired.

4. Using a vegetable peeler, shave along the side of the white chocolate bar and the milk chocolate bar to make chocolate curls and shavings. Sprinkle over the top of each mug.

Makes: 5 (6 ounce) servings

Snickerdoodle Cocoa

Equipment list:

- heavy medium pot
- measuring spoons and cups
- whisk or wooden spoon
- ladle
- mugs

Ingredient list:

- 8 tablespoons sugar
- 8 teaspoons cocoa powder
- 1 teaspoon salt
- 4 cups milk
- 1 teaspoon pure vanilla extract
- 1 cup cinnamon chips or 2½ teaspoons ground cinnamon

This cocoa has the cinnamony taste of the cookie that this drink is named for, with all the creamy goodness and warmth of hot cocoa.

1. Place the sugar, cocoa powder, salt, milk and vanilla into a heavy medium pot.

2. Cook over low heat until the mixture is smooth and blended. Use a whisk or wooden spoon to stir as it cooks. Make sure the heat stays low so the milk doesn't burn.

3. To serve, ladle the hot cocoa into mugs. Top each mug with ¼ cup of the cinnamon chips or ½ teaspoon ground cinnamon. Stir to help the chips melt.

Makes: 5 (6 ounce) servings

...pment list:

- ...measuring cups and spoons
- electric blender
- tall glasses

Ingredient list:

- 4 cups vanilla ice cream or frozen yogurt
- 2 cups orange juice
- 4 tablespoons milk
- 6 tablespoons sugar
- 2 teaspoons pure vanilla extract

When I was a kid, the ice cream truck used to drive though my neighborhood just at dessert time. He would ring his bells and kids would come running out of every front door with a fistful of quarters. I have been known to eat a creamsicle or 2 (or 100!) in my day.

For a pretty decoration, cut 6 thin orange slices. Place the slices on a piece of parchment paper and into the freezer. When they are frozen, slit a corner and hang a frozen orange slice off the rim of each glass.

1. Place the ice cream, orange juice, milk, sugar, and vanilla into a blender. Place the cover on the blender.

2. Blend until smooth. Pour into tall glasses.

Makes: 6 servings

Root Beer Floats

Dairy

Equipment list:

- 4 tall glasses
- ice cream scooper
- 4 salad or dessert plates
- measuring cups

Ingredient list:

- hot fudge or chocolate sauce from a jar or bottle
- 1 pint vanilla ice cream
- 2 (8-ounce) cans or bottles of root beer, cold
- whipped cream
- maraschino cherries

Make sure that your root beer is nice and cold when you begin the recipe or it will melt the ice cream too quickly. Root beer floats are sometimes called "Black Cows". To make a "Brown Cow" substitute cola for the root beer.

1. Squeeze or spoon some hot fudge or chocolate sauce into each glass.

2. Place 1 scoop of vanilla ice cream into each glass. Place each glass onto a salad or dessert plate to catch the fizzy overflow. Pour root beer over the ice cream to just cover it. Add a second scoop of ice cream. Add more root beer to cover. Watch the ice cream float to the top. If you have room you can add another scoop of ice cream and more root beer.

3. Top with whipped cream, hot fudge or chocolate sauce, and a maraschino cherry.

Makes: 4 servings

Thick & Rich Milkshakes

Dairy

Equipment list:

- measuring cups and spoons
- electric blender
- tall glasses

Ingredient list:

- 2 cups vanilla, chocolate or strawberry ice cream or frozen yogurt
- ½ cup milk
- ½ cup heavy cream
- 1 teaspoon vanilla extract

This is my husband's specialty, the kind of milkshake that leaves a serious milk mustache. His secret ingredient is that he adds a few squares of milk chocolate to his chocolate milkshakes and white chocolate to his vanilla ones right before he turns on the blender.

1. Place the ice cream, milk, heavy cream, and vanilla into a blender. Place the cover on the blender.

2. Blend until smooth. If you like thinner milkshakes, blend for a longer time. If you like thicker shakes, blend for a shorter time and you can add more ice cream. Pour into glasses and serve.

Makes: 2 servings

Lemonade

Equipment list:

- measuring cups
- small pot
- whisk or wooden spoon
- cutting board
- sharp knife
- 2-cup liquid measuring cup
- strainer
- pitcher
- glasses

Ingredient list:

- 2 cups sugar
- 1 cup water
- juice of 8-10 lemons
- 7 cups cold water
- ice cubes

With this recipe and a fun sign, your lemonade stand business will be booming.

For a unique twist, whip up a batch of frozen lemonade! Just prepare the recipe as below. Fill a blender with ice. Add 1 cup of the prepared lemonade and blend. You can add a drop or 2 of yellow food coloring to pump up the color.

1. Place the sugar and 1 cup of water into a small pot.

2. Bring to a boil over medium heat and stir with a whisk or wooden spoon until the sugar dissolves.

3. Place this pot of sugar water into the refrigerator to cool down.

4. Place the lemons on your cutting board. Roll them, pressing down to loosen the juice.

5. Using a sharp knife, cut each lemon in half.

6. Squeeze the juice into a 2-cup liquid measuring cup. You will need 1½ cups of lemon juice. Set aside.

7. Pour the lemon juice through a strainer, into a pitcher, discarding any pits.

8. Add the cooled sugar water and the 7 cups of cold water to the pitcher. Add in ice cubes and stir. Pour into glasses.

Makes: 8-10 servings

Desserts

Chocolate Chip Cookie Dough Cheesecake

Equipment list:

- large heavy-duty Ziploc® bag
- rolling pin (optional)
- medium mixing bowl
- microwave-safe bowl
- microwave
- silicone spatula
- 9-inch springform pan
- measuring cups and spoons
- electric mixer and bowl
- knife or offset spatula

Ingredient list:

- 2 (8-ounce) blocks of cream cheese (not whipped)
- 1 (1-pound) bag store-bought chocolate chip cookies, divided, similar size to Chips Ahoy®
- 6 tablespoons butter
- 1 cup sugar
- 1 cup sour cream
- 4 large eggs
- 2 teaspoons pure vanilla extract
- ½ cup cookie dough
- garnish: 3 tablespoons sour cream and 1 extra chocolate chip cookie from the package

You can buy cookie dough in the refrigerator section of the supermarket. Just break or slice off enough to fill the ½ cup measuring cup. If you can't find the pre-made dough, whip up half a batch of your favorite chocolate chip cookie recipe and measure out a half-cup of dough.

1. Preheat the oven to 350° F.

2. Open up the packages of cream cheese and let the cream cheese soften at room temperature.

3. Meanwhile, place 29 of the chocolate chip cookies into the Ziploc® bag. Make sure you save 1 cookie for the top decoration. Using a rolling pin or just your hands, crush the cookies into crumbs. Pour the crumbs into a medium bowl.

4. Place the butter into a microwave-safe bowl. Microwave for 45 seconds or until it is melted. Pour the butter over the cookie crumbs and toss with the spatula or your fingers to coat the crumbs with the melted butter.

5. Make sure your base is locked into place on your springform pan. Use your hands to pat the buttered cookie crumbs into the bottom of the springform pan.

6. Stand 12-13 cookies around the inside edge of the pan, flat side facing in, pressing them firmly into the crumbs so that they stand and don't fall over. Set aside.

7. Place the cream cheese and sugar into the bowl of an electric mixer. Beat the cream cheese and sugar until creamy. Add in the sour cream, eggs, and vanilla and beat until smooth. Pour the cream cheese mixture into the prepared crust. Use your silicone spatula to get it all out of the mixing bowl.

8. Roll the cookie dough into 1-inch balls. Drop the balls into and all around the cream cheese batter, making sure the batter covers the top of each cookie dough ball.

9. Place into the oven and bake for 50 minutes. Without opening the door, turn off the oven and let the cheesecake stay in the oven for an extra hour. Remove the cake from the oven and let it cool on the counter or table for at least 1 hour. Spread the 3 tablespoons of sour cream in a circle in the center, and place a chocolate chip cookie in the center of the sour cream.

10. Place the cheesecake into the refrigerator for a few hours or overnight.

11. When you are ready to serve, using a small offset spatula or thin knife, go around the inside of the pan to loosen the cookies from the sides. Open the spring and remove the sides of the springform pan. Cut into slices.

Makes: 10-12 servings

Quick and Easy Chocolate Cake

Dairy or Parve

Equipment list:

- 8 or 9-inch round baking pan
- measuring cups and spoons
- large mixing bowl
- wooden spoon or silicone spatula
- electric mixer
- toothpick
- dull knife or thin metal spatula
- wire rack
- 2 forks
- small sieve

Ingredient list:

- nonstick cooking spray with flour in it, like Pam® or Baker's Joy®
- 1 cup all-purpose flour
- 1 cup sugar
- ½ cup unsweetened cocoa powder
- ½ teaspoon baking soda
- ¼ teaspoon baking powder
- ¼ teaspoon salt
- 1 cup milk, or soymilk
- ⅓ cup canola or vegetable oil
- 1 teaspoon pure vanilla extract
- 1 large egg
- confectioner's sugar

1. Preheat the oven to 350° F.

2. With the can of nonstick cooking spray, coat the baking pan. If you only have the spray without the flour, spray the pan, then add 2 teaspoons of flour into it. Shake it over a garbage can to get it all around and to shake out the extra.

3. In the large mixing bowl, use a wooden spoon or silicone spatula to combine the flour, sugar, cocoa powder, baking soda, baking powder, and salt.

4. Add the milk or soymilk, oil, and vanilla. Crack the egg and add it to the bowl.

5. Beat with an electric mixer for 3 minutes until all combined and the batter is creamy.

6. Pour the batter into the prepared pan.

7. Place the pan into the oven and bake for 30 minutes. When you stick a toothpick into the center of the cake, it should come out clean. If it is not clean bake another 5 minutes.

8. Remove the cake from the oven and let it cool for 10 minutes in the pan.

9. Using a dull knife or thin metal spatula, go around the rim of the cake to loosen it from the pan. Turn the pan over and remove the cake. Let it cool completely on a wire rack. This will help air circulate to both sides and cool it properly.

10. When you are ready to serve the cake, lay 2 forks criss-crossed across the top of the cake.

11. Place the confectioner's sugar into a small sieve. Tap it over the top of the cake.

12. Carefully lift up the forks. You will be left with a pretty design.

Makes: 8-10 servings

Confetti Cake

Equipment list:

- 8-inch square baking pan
- measuring cups and spoons
- large mixing bowl
- microwave-safe bowl or small pot
- microwave
- electric mixer
- silicone spatula
- toothpick
- dull knife or thin metal spatula
- wire rack

Ingredient list:

- nonstick cooking spray with flour in it, like Pam® or Baker's Joy®
- 1 cup all-purpose flour
- 1 cup sugar
- 1 teaspoon baking powder
- ¼ teaspoon salt
- ⅔ cup milk, or soymilk
- 1 teaspoon pure vanilla extract
- 1 large egg
- 4 tablespoons (¼ cup) butter or margarine
- 3 tablespoons colored non-pareils
- vanilla frosting (optional)

Non-pareils are the small, round colored sprinkles. They can turn any plain cake into a celebration!

1. Preheat the oven to 350° F.

2. With the can of nonstick cooking spray, coat the baking pan. If you only have the spray without the flour, spray the pan, then add 2 teaspoons of flour into it. Shake it over a garbage can to get it all around and to shake out the extra.

3. In the large mixing bowl, combine the flour, sugar, baking powder, and salt.

4. Add the milk or soymilk and the vanilla.

5. Crack the egg and add it to the bowl.

6. Melt the butter or margarine either in a microwave-safe bowl for 45 seconds or in a small pot over medium heat. Allow the melted butter or margarine to cool for 5 minutes so it doesn't melt the non-pareils when you add them. Add the melted butter or margarine to the batter. Beat for 3 minutes.

7. Add the non-pareils.

8. Beat with an electric mixer until just combined and creamy. Scrape down the sides with a silicone spatula.

9. Pour the batter into the prepared pan.

10. Place the pan into the oven and bake for 30-35 minutes. When you stick a toothpick into the center of the cake, it should come out clean.

11. Remove the cake from the oven and let it cool for 10 minutes in the pan.

12. Use a dull knife or thin metal spatula. Go around the rim of the cake to loosen it from the pan. Turn the pan over and remove the cake. Let it cool completely on a wire rack. This will help air circulate to both sides and cool it properly.

13. If you would like, frost with vanilla frosting and shake on a few more non-pareils.

Makes: 8-10 servings

Cookies-n-Creamwiches

Equipment list:

- 2 cookie sheets
- parchment paper
- 2 medium mixing bowls
- measuring cups and spoons
- electric mixer
- fork
- ruler
- offset spatula
- sharp knife

Ingredient list:

- 3 pints favorite flavor ice cream or parve ice cream
- 2 sticks (1 cup) butter or margarine
- 1½ cups sugar
- 1½ cups dark brown sugar
- 4 large eggs
- 1 tablespoon pure vanilla extract
- 4½ cups all-purpose flour
- 2 teaspoons baking soda
- 1 teaspoon salt
- 1 (12-ounce) bag semi-sweet chocolate chips
- toppings: assorted sprinkles, chocolate chips, chopped nuts, chopped up candy bars

I scream, you scream, we'll all scream for ice cream, especially when it's served in such a cool way!

1. Place the pints of ice cream into the refrigerator to soften while you work.

2. Turn the oven to 375° F.

3. Let the butter or margarine sit at room temperature for 15 minutes, or place it in the microwave for 15 seconds to soften it.

4. Line the cookie sheets with parchment paper.

5. Place the softened butter or margarine into a mixing bowl. Add the sugar and brown sugar. With the electric mixer at medium speed, beat the mixture until it is smooth and creamy.

6. Add the eggs and beat until fluffy. Add the vanilla and beat until it is mixed in.

7. Place the flour, baking soda, and salt into a mixing bowl. With a fork, mix them together. Gradually add this flour mixture to the creamed mixture. Beat for 1 minute. Sprinkle in the chocolate chips and mix them in.

8. Divide the dough in half, and place each half on one of the prepared cookie sheets. Use your palms to spread each piece of dough into a large, flattened circle. Use a ruler, to measure the flattened dough so that each cookie is about 12 inches wide.

9. Place the cookie sheets into the oven and bake for 20 minutes.

10. Remove the cookie sheets from the oven; slide the

parchment paper off the cookie sheet and allow the cookies to cool for 20 minutes.

11. Remove the ice cream from the refrigerator.

12. Gently turn one of the cookies upside down (so the flat side is facing up) and spread the ice cream into a 2-inch layer. Use an offset spatula to help you spread it. Running the spatula under hot water before spreading, helps spread the ice cream more easily. Top the giant creamwiches with the 2nd cookie, flat side down. Place the cookie into the freezer so that the ice cream will become firm.

13. Remove the cookie from the freezer. Have a grown-up help slice it into wedges; you need a strong knife. If the ice cream is too soft, place the wedges onto a cookie sheet and into the freezer, uncovered, to firm up again.

14. Place your toppings, such as sprinkles, mini chocolate chips, chopped up candy bars, etc., into separate plates.

15. Pick up each wedge and decorate the outside of the creamwiches by dipping each of the 3 exposed sides into a different topping of your choice. Place the wedges back into the freezer to get firm.

Makes: 8-10 giant wedges

Chocolate Fudge Truffles

Dairy

Equipment list:

- measuring cups and spoons
- medium pot
- whisk
- can opener
- silicone spatula or wooden spoon
- bowl
- paper petit four cups

Ingredient list:

- 4 tablespoons cocoa powder
- 1 cup whole milk
- 1 cup sweetened condensed milk, from a small can
- 1 tablespoon butter
- assorted sprinkles
- non-pareils
- cocoa powder
- confectioner's sugar (powdered sugar)

My Brazillian friend, Arlette, who taught me this recipe told me that she has never been to a party in Brazil where these truffles were not served. My kids call these "little balls of frozen hot fudge." They are rich, creamy, and fudgey. They taste best served cold.

1. Measure the cocoa powder into a medium pot. Add the milk and whisk.

2. Use your can opener to open the can of sweetened condensed milk. Measure out 1 cup and pour it into the pot.

3. Turn the heat to medium, add the butter and cook the mixture, slowly stirring with the spatula or wooden spoon almost the whole time. Make sure the mixture doesn't rise up over the sides. It will bubble as it thickens and cooks, just make sure it doesn't rise. If you see this happening, lift the pot off the heat from the handle for 2-3 seconds, lower the flame, and return the pot to the heat. Cook for 20-28 minutes. The mixture will thicken, and when you tilt the pan, the truffle mixture will not be runny. When you scoop up the chocolate it will not drip off the spatula. Go by the thickness more than the timing. You want it thick like frosting.

4. Using your spatula, scoop the mixture into a bowl and place in the refrigerator to cool for 20 minutes.

5. When the mixture is completely cool, rub some butter on the palms of your hands.

6. Using a teaspoon measure, scoop out 1 teaspoon of truffle batter into your hand and gently roll it into a ball.

7. Roll each ball in either sprinkles, non-pareils, cocoa, or confectioner's sugar.

8. Place the truffles in small paper petit four cups.

9. Place into the refrigerator. Serve them cold.

Makes: 25-30 truffles

Oatmeal Raisinette Cookies

Dairy or Parve

Equipment list:

- 2 cookie sheets
- parchment paper
- large mixing bowl
- measuring cups and spoons
- electric mixer
- small mixing bowl
- silicone spatula or wooden spoon
- fork
- metal spatula
- wire rack

Ingredient list:

- 1½ cups (2½ sticks) unsalted butter or margarine, at room temperature for 20 minutes
- ¾ cup dark brown sugar
- ½ cup sugar
- 1 large egg
- 1 teaspoon pure vanilla extract
- 1½ cups all-purpose flour
- 1 teaspoon baking soda
- 1 teaspoon cinnamon
- ¾ cup old fashioned oats (not the quick cooking or instant type)
- 1 cup chocolate covered raisins

For a parve version of this recipe, you can use plain raisins or sweetened dried cranberries like Craisins®. I like using chocolate-covered raisins. They make a cookie that is a cross between chocolate chip and oatmeal raisin, my two all-time favorites.

1. Preheat the oven to 375° F.

2. Line the cookie sheets with parchment paper. Set aside.

3. Place the butter or margarine into a large mixing bowl. Pack the brown sugar into the measuring cup and dump it into the bowl. Add the sugar.

4. With your electric mixer, beat the butter with the sugars until smooth and creamy.

5. Add the egg and vanilla to the sugar mixture and use your mixer to combine.

6. In a small bowl, mix the flour, baking soda, and cinnamon. Mix with a fork to combine.

7. Add the flour mixture into the sugar mixture and beat to combine.

8. With your spatula or wooden spoon, mix in the oats and the chocolate covered raisins.

9. Scoop out tablespoon sized balls of the batter and place on the prepared cookie sheets. Allow 3 inches between each cookie for the cookies to spread.

10. Place in the oven and bake for 12-13 minutes.

11. When the cookies are done, remove them from

the oven. Let them cool for 5 minutes and then, with a metal spatula, move them to a rack to cool completely.

Makes: 40 cookies

Vanilla Grape Tart

Equipment list:

- 9-inch springform pan
- food processor
- measuring cups and spoons
- knife
- small offset spatula
- electric mixer
- cutting board
- spoon
- small sieve

Ingredient list:

- nonstick cooking spray
- 1 cup all-purpose flour
- 3 tablespoons sugar
- ½ teaspoon salt
- 8 tablespoons (1 stick) unsalted butter or margarine
- 2 tablespoons very cold water
- ½ cup graham cracker crumbs
- 1¼ cups cold milk or soymilk
- 1 (3.4 ounce) box instant pudding and pie filling powder (make sure it is instant)
- 1 tablespoon pure vanilla extract
- 1 cup red seedless grapes
- 1 cup green seedless grapes
- 1 tablespoon confectioner's sugar

If you want to wow your family with a Shabbat or holiday dessert, this is a winner. Just follow the ingredients for parve. This tart is best when grapes are sweet and in season.

As an added bonus, you can use this crust and pudding to make a Banana Cream Pie. Just leave off the grapes, add a layer of whipped cream, and place some sliced bananas on top.

1. Preheat the oven to 375° F.

2. Spray the bottom of the springform pan with nonstick cooking spray. Try not to get it on the sides of the pan. Set aside.

3. Attach the bowl to the food processor. Place the metal blade on the food processor.

4. Place the flour, sugar, and salt into the bowl of the food processor.

5. With your knife, slice the stick of butter or margarine into 8 pieces and add them to the bowl of the food processor.

6. Attach the lid and pulse to combine the ingredients. Through the small hole in the lid or cover, add the cold water. Pulse until it forms a ball of dough.

7. Open the lid and add the graham cracker crumbs. Pulse for 1 minute until most of the crumbs are part of the dough ball.

8. Press the dough into the bottom of the pan using a small offset spatula or the palm of your hand. Use your palm to get it smooth and work it up the sides of the pan by about 2 inches.

9. Place the crust into the oven and bake for 20-25 minutes until golden brown.

10. Remove the crust from the oven and let it cool for 20 minutes.

11. Prepare the filling. Place the milk or soymilk, pudding mix, and vanilla into the bowl of an electric mixer. Beat for 4 minutes or until thickened. Spoon the filling into the crust.

12. On your cutting board, with a knife, slice each grape in half. Make a ring of green grapes, cut side down, around the outside rim of the tart. Make a ring of red grapes inside the green ring. Follow with a ring of green grapes. Continue doing this until there is no more room for grapes. You may have extra grapes.

13. Place the tart into the refrigerator for at least 20 minutes, or up to 1 day in advance.

14. When ready to serve the tart, release the sides of the springform pan and place the tart on a plate.

15. Place the confectioner's sugar in a small sieve and tap it over the tart.

Makes: 10-12 servings

White Chocolate Mousse in Chocolate Boxes

Dairy

Equipment list:

- 2 microwave-safe bowls
- microwave
- 2 silicone spatulas
- electric mixer with whisk attachment and bowl
- small paintbrush
- vegetable peeler

Ingredient list:

Mousse:

- 4 ounces good quality white chocolate, broken into small pieces
- ½ cup heavy cream
- 3 tablespoons confectioner's sugar

Chocolate boxes:

- 2-3 (4-ounce) milk chocolate bars

Most chocolate bars have indent or score marks. Use these as guides to help break your chocolate into 4 even squares to build your box out of.

1. Place the white chocolate in a microwave-safe bowl. Microwave for 45 seconds. Stir with a silicone spatula. Return the bowl to the microwave and microwave for 30-35 seconds more. When you remove the bowl and stir again, it should be all melted. Let the chocolate cool for 5 minutes.

2. If your mixer has a whisk attachment, use it here. Place the heavy cream and confectioner's sugar into the bowl of a mixer. Beat at high speed until it is whipped, fluffy and stiff. When you run a spatula through the center, it should leave a mark. If it doesn't, whip it a little longer.

3. With your spatula, scoop the white chocolate into the cream. Beat it in with the mixer for 10 seconds. Place the bowl into the refrigerator.

4. Make your chocolate boxes. Break each milk chocolate bar so that you have 4 equal square walls (the amount of squares will depend on what your chocolate bar looks like).

5. Take two of the extra squares (or 2 tablespoons chocolate chips, if you have no extra squares) and place them in a microwave-safe bowl. Microwave for 60 seconds. Stir with a silicone spatula. Return the bowl to the microwave and microwave for 30-

35 seconds more. When you remove and stir it again, it should be all melted.

6. Carefully remove the melted chocolate. Build your chocolate boxes on a plate so that you can easily move them to the refrigerator. With a paintbrush, use the melted chocolate as the "glue" to attach the 4 chocolate walls together to make a box. Make sure your smooth sides are facing in. Repeat with the second chocolate bar. Place the boxes in the refrigerator to firm up for 5 minutes.

7. Fill each chocolate box with the white chocolate mousse.

8. Hold some of the extra chocolate over the top of the mousse. Run a vegetable peeler over the chocolate to make shavings that fall onto the mousse.

Makes: 2 servings

Sugar Cookies

Equipment list:

- 2 cookie sheets
- parchment paper
- measuring cups and spoons
- medium mixing bowl
- fork
- large mixing bowl
- electric mixer
- rolling pin
- 3-inch round cookie cutter
- metal spatula
- assorted slotted spatulas or other flat kitchen utensils that have openings
- wire rack

Ingredient list:

- 8 tablespoons (1 stick) unsalted butter or margarine
- 2 cups all-purpose flour
- 2 teaspoons baking powder
- ½ teaspoon salt
- 1 cup sugar
- 1 large egg
- 2 tablespoons orange juice
- 1 teaspoon pure vanilla extract
- nonstick cooking spray, like Pam®
- assorted colored sanding sugar

1. Preheat the oven to 375° F.

2. Let the margarine or butter soften at room temperature for 15 minutes.

3. Line the cookie sheets with parchment paper. Set aside.

4. Place the flour, baking powder, and salt into a medium mixing bowl. Stir with a fork to mix. Set these dry ingredients aside.

5. Place the softened butter or margarine into the large mixing bowl. Add the sugar. Beat with an electric mixer until creamy and fluffy. Add in the egg, orange juice, and vanilla. Beat to combine.

6. Sprinkle in the mixture of dry ingredients. Beat until all combined.

7. Spread out a sheet of parchment paper on your work surface. Transfer the dough onto the parchment paper. Top with a second sheet of parchment paper; this will keep the rolling pin from sticking to the dough.

8. With the rolling pin, roll the dough into a thin even layer a little less than ¼ inch thick. Remove the top sheet of parchment paper. Use your cookie cutter to cut out round cookies. Transfer the cookies with your metal spatula to the prepared cookie sheets. Re-roll the scraps of dough and continue to cut out cookies until the dough is used up. If the dough becomes too soft, place it into the refrigerator to firm up.

9. Spray the tops of the cookies with nonstick cooking spray. Take your spatula or other kitchen tool and rest it on one cookie. Sprinkle with one

color of the sanding sugar. Carefully lift the spatula or tool away. Repeat with different kitchen tools and various colored sugars.

10. Place the cookies into the hot oven and bake for 10 minutes.

11. Carefully remove the cookie sheets from the oven and transfer the cookies to a wire rack.

Makes: 24 cookies

Apple Crisp

Equipment list:

- vegetable peeler
- cutting board
- sharp knife
- melon baller
- large mixing bowl
- 8-inch square or round baking dish or individual ramekins
- measuring cups and spoons
- medium mixing bowl
- wooden spoon

Ingredient list:

- 4 medium apples
- ½ lemon
- ⅓ cup sugar
- 2 tablespoons flour
- ½ teaspoon cinnamon
- 1 tablespoon apricot preserves
- ½ cup all-purpose flour
- ½ cup dark brown sugar
- ½ cup old fashioned oats (not instant or quick cooking type)
- ½ cup chopped pecans or walnuts
- ½ teaspoon cinnamon
- 8 tablespoons butter or margarine, softened at room temperature for 15 minutes

My favorite apples for crisps are Granny Smith, Braeburn, and Northern Spy. Feel free to try this recipe with any of these varieties or use more than one kind at a time.

1. Preheat the oven to 375° F.

2. Prepare the filling. Peel the apples. On your cutting board, with a sharp knife, cut each apple in half. Use your melon baller to scoop out the seeds and the stem. Slice each apple half into ¼-inch thin slices.

3. Place the apples into a large mixing bowl. Squeeze the lemon half over the apples, catching the seeds in your hand. Discard the seeds. Toss the apples with the ⅓ cup sugar, 2 tablespoons flour, and ½ teaspoon cinnamon. Dot the top of the apples with the apricot preserves.

4. Empty the apples into an 8-inch baking dish or individual ramekins.

5. Prepare the topping. In a medium mixing bowl, mix the flour, brown sugar, oats, nuts, and cinnamon.

6. On your cutting board, with a sharp knife, cut the butter or margarine into 16 pieces.

7. Add the butter or margarine pieces into the mixing bowl. With your fingers, rub in the butter so that it makes big crumbs of topping.

8. Sprinkle the crumb topping over the top of the apples. Spread it out evenly with a wooden spoon.

9. Place the apple crisp into the hot oven and bake uncovered for 45 minutes. The top will be brown and the apples will be soft.

10. Serve the crisp warm. Scoop out portions of the crisp onto your dessert plates. You can top each plate with a scoop of vanilla ice cream.

Makes: 9 servings

Chocolate Haystacks

Equipment list:

- cookie sheet
- parchment paper
- medium pot
- silicone spatula
- measuring spoons
- soup spoon

Ingredient list:

- 7-8 ounces good quality white chocolate, milk chocolate, or semi-sweet chocolate
- ½ cup dry roasted peanuts
- 2-3 handfuls of thin pretzel sticks

The most important ingredient in this recipe is the chocolate. Make sure you are using good quality chocolate bars, the kind you want to snack on. Try not to use parve chocolate chips; they don't tend to be made out of good tasting chocolate. I like the Belgian and Israeli brands of chocolate bars, like Schmerling and Elite. Ghirardelli white chocolate bars work well too. They usually come in 3½- or 4-ounce bars so you will need two bars to make this recipe.

1. Line the cookie sheet with parchment paper. Set aside.

2. Break the chocolate up into small pieces. Most chocolate bars have score marks and you can use them as your guide. Place the chocolate into a medium pot.

3. Turn the heat to low. Melt the chocolate, stirring the whole time with a silicone spatula. Chocolate burns easily and can be tricky to work with. Every 45 seconds, lift the pot off the heat and give the chocolate a good stir to help it melt more quickly.

4. If for some reason your chocolate is not smooth or shiny, add 2 tablespoons of water and return the pot to the heat, stirring the whole time to make it smooth.

5. Remove the pot from the heat.

6. Add the peanuts into the pot.

7. Break the pretzel sticks in half and add them to the pot.

8. Use your silicone spatula and stir to coat the peanuts and pretzels.

9. Using a soup spoon, scoop out spoonfuls of the mixture. Place the "haystacks" on the prepared cookie sheet.

10. Place into the refrigerator for 15-20 minutes or until the chocolate has hardened.

11. Store the haystacks in an airtight container in the pantry or in the refrigerator.

Makes: 9 haystacks

Chocolate Chip Crunch Cookies

Dairy or Parve

Equipment list:

- cookie sheet
- parchment paper
- microwave-safe bowl
- microwave
- medium mixing bowl
- measuring cups and spoons
- electric mixer
- silicone spatula or wooden spoon
- metal spatula
- wire rack

Ingredient list:

- ½ cup (1 stick) butter or margarine
- ½ cup sugar
- ¼ cup dark brown sugar
- 1 large egg
- 1 teaspoon pure vanilla extract
- 1 cup all-purpose flour
- ½ teaspoon baking soda
- ½ teaspoon baking powder
- ¼ teaspoon salt
- 1 cup crisp rice cereal like Rice Krispies®
- 1 cup chocolate chips

This is a really good chocolate chip cookie with a little extra crunch.

1. Preheat the oven to 350° F.

2. Line the cookie sheet with parchment paper. Set aside.

3. Place the butter or margarine in a microwave-safe bowl and microwave it for 45 seconds to melt it. You can also melt it in a small pot over medium heat.

4. Pour the melted butter or margarine into a medium mixing bowl.

5. Add the sugar and brown sugar.

6. With an electric mixer, beat until fluffy.

7. Add the egg and vanilla. Beat until smooth.

8. Add in the flour, baking soda, baking powder, and salt. Mix to combine.

9. With a silicone spatula or wooden spoon, mix in the crisp rice cereal and chocolate chips. Stir the batter until it is all combined.

10. Using a tablespoon sized measuring spoon, scoop out mounds of dough and place them on the prepared cookie sheet.

11. Place the tray in the oven and bake for 10-12 minutes.

12. Remove the cookie sheets from the oven. Allow the

cookies to cool for 3-4 minutes. Remove the cookies with a metal spatula to a rack to cool completely.

13. Repeat until all of the dough is used up.

Makes: 30 cookies

Meringue Surprise Kisses

Parve

Equipment list:

- 2 cookie sheets
- parchment paper
- measuring cups and spoons
- electric mixer and bowl
- silicone spatula
- heavy-duty gallon size Ziploc® bag
- scissors

Ingredient list:

- 4 large egg whites
- 1 teaspoon cornstarch
- 2½ cups confectioner's sugar
- ¼ cup chocolate chips

Meringue cookies are so simple to make. They just need patience, both to prepare and to bake. The chocolate chips are a sweet surprise in the center that stay hidden until the cookie is eaten.

1. Preheat the oven to 225° F.

2. Line 2 cookie sheets with parchment paper. Set aside.

3. Place the egg whites and cornstarch into the bowl of a mixer. Beat the egg whites with the mixer on medium high speed for a full 5 minutes.

4. With the machine running the entire time sprinkle in the confectioner's sugar a little at a time as you beat it at medium high for a full 10-12 minutes. When you lift the beaters, the meringue should hold its shape as a stiff peak off the tip of the beaters. It will be very shiny.

5. Roll down the top of the Ziploc® bag, 2 or 3 rolls. This will make a cuff on the outside of the bag.

6. Using a silicone spatula, transfer the meringue from the mixing bowl into the bag.

7. Unroll the cuff and twist the top a few times, to close the bag and force the meringue into the bottom of the bag.

8. With your scissors, snip a small corner off of the bag. Squeeze 1½ inch circles of meringue onto the cookie sheets. If it is coming out too slowly, snip the hole a little bigger.

9. Place 3 chocolate chips into the center of each meringue.

10. Top each cookie with a squeeze of meringue to cover the chocolate chips. If you squeeze slowly and then pull the tip up you will get a pretty top like a chocolate kiss.

11. Place into the oven and bake for 2 hours.

12. When the cookies are done, lift them off the parchment. If they stick at all, return them to the oven for another 30 minutes to finish drying out.

Makes: 20-24 kisses

Chocolate Pudding

Dairy

Equipment list:

- measuring cups and spoons
- medium pot
- whisk
- silicone spatula
- medium mixing bowl
- plastic wrap

Ingredient list:

- ¾ cup sugar
- 2 tablespoons cornstarch
- 3 tablespoons Dutch process cocoa powder
- ⅛ teaspoon salt
- 2 cups milk
- 1 cup heavy cream
- 2 large egg yolks
- ½ cups semi-sweet chocolate chips
- ½ teaspoon pure vanilla extract
- 1 tablespoon butter
- whipped cream

1. Place the sugar, cornstarch, cocoa, and salt into a medium pot. Whisk to combine.

2. Add the milk, cream, and egg yolks. Whisk again to combine. Add the chocolate chips.

3. Place the pot over medium heat. Let the mixture cook for 12-15 minutes, whisking almost the whole time. Use your silicone spatula to scrape the edges of the pot into the center. Make sure your heat is not too high or the milk will burn. The mixture should start to boil a little and it will get a little thicker. You want the mixture to look like a thick pudding. Go by the look more than the time, because everyone's stove heats differently.

4. Turn off the heat and whisk in the vanilla and butter. Mix until the butter is melted.

5. Pour the pudding into a medium mixing bowl. Allow it to stand for 5 minutes to cool off a bit.

6. Hang a piece of plastic wrap over the top of the bowl, allowing it to touch the surface of the pudding; this will keep a skin from forming on the pudding.

7. Place in the refrigerator to cool for at least 2 hours. The pudding will thicken as it cools.

8. Serve with whipped cream.

M akes: 6 servings

Fudgey Brownies

Equipment list:

- 8- by 12-inch brownie pan
- measuring cups and spoons
- medium pot
- whisk
- silicone spatula or wooden spoon
- electric mixer and bowl

Ingredient list:

- nonstick cooking spray
- 12 ounces good quality semi-sweet chocolate bars
- 6 tablespoons butter or margarine
- ⅔ cup sugar
- 2 tablespoons water
- 2 large eggs
- 1 teaspoon pure vanilla extract
- ¾ cup all-purpose flour
- ½ teaspoon baking soda
- ½ teaspoon salt

Frosting:

- 3 tablespoons butter or margarine
- 3 tablespoons cocoa powder
- 1 tablespoon light corn syrup
- 1 teaspoon pure vanilla extract
- 1 cup confectioner's sugar
- 1½ tablespoons milk or soymilk

The most important ingredient in this recipe is the chocolate. Make sure you are using good quality chocolate bars. The better the chocolate, the better the brownies will be. The frosting is optional; they are great with or without it.

1. Preheat the oven to 325° F.

2. Spray the brownie pan with nonstick cooking spray. Set aside.

3. Break the chocolate bars into small pieces. They are usually scored so just break them up on the lines. Set aside.

4. Place the butter or margarine into a medium pot. Add the sugar and water.

5. Cook over medium heat until the butter or margarine is melted and the mixture just starts to boil.

6. Remove the pot from the heat. Add in the chocolate and whisk to help the chocolate melt.

7. Whisk in the eggs, one at a time. Whisk in the vanilla.

8. Add in the flour, baking soda, and salt. With a silicone spatula or wooden spoon, mix until all of the ingredients are mixed in; it will be too thick to whisk.

9. Pour the batter into the prepared pan.

10. Place the pan into the hot oven and bake for 30 minutes. To keep them fudgey, do not over bake. If you bake it longer you will get a cakier brownie.

11. Allow the brownies to cool for 5 minutes. Place the pan into the refrigerator to cool. Serve the brownies chilled.

12. To make the frosting: Place the butter or margarine, cocoa powder, corn syrup, and vanilla into a medium mixing bowl. With an electric mixer, beat until it is mixed well. Add the confectioner's sugar and the milk or soymilk. Beat it until it looks like frosting. Spread evenly over the brownies. Cut into squares.

Makes: 12 brownies

Lemon Lime Bars

Dairy or Parve

Equipment list:

- 13 x 9 x 2 inch baking pan
- measuring cups and spoons
- knife
- large mixing bowl
- medium mixing bowl
- whisk
- microplane or box grater
- cutting board
- small bowl
- sifter or small sieve

Ingredient list:

- nonstick cooking spray
- 1½ cups all-purpose flour
- ⅔ cup confectioner's sugar
- 1½ sticks (12 tablespoons) butter or margarine
- 5 large eggs
- 1¾ cups sugar
- 6 tablespoons all-purpose flour
- 1 teaspoon baking powder
- 4 limes
- 3 lemons
- ½ cup confectioner's sugar for the top

The colored skin of a lemon or lime is called zest. It adds a lot of flavor in baking. Whether you are using a microplane zester or the small holes of a box grater, make sure you only get the yellow or green zest. The next layer, which is white, is called pith, and it is very bitter.

1. Preheat oven to 350° F.

2. Spray the baking pan with nonstick cooking spray.

3. Place the flour and ⅔ cup confectioner's sugar into a large bowl.

4. Unwrap your butter or margarine. With a knife, cut the butter or margarine into small pieces. Add them to the flour.

5. With your fingertips, knead the mixture until it begins to come together. It won't be a smooth dough but it will hold together.

6. With wet palms, press the dough evenly into the prepared pan. Place the pan into the hot oven and bake for 20 minutes.

7. While the crust is baking, prepare the filling.

8. Crack the eggs into a medium mixing bowl. Whisk them until they are bright yellow.

9. Add the 1¾ cups of sugar, 6 tablespoons of flour, and the baking powder. Whisk again.

10. With your hands, roll each lemon and lime on your countertop to release the juices.

11. Hold a microplane or the side of a grater that has the small holes over the egg mixture. Carefully

rub the lemon or lime back and forth and remove the zest from ½ of a lemon and ½ of a lime. Stop when you get to the white layer under the colored skin. Whisk in this zest.

12. On your cutting board, with a sharp knife, cut each lime and lemon in half. Squeeze as much juice as you can from them into a small bowl. Don't do it directly into the egg mixture or you may end up having some pits sneak into the batter that you don't see. Remove any pits and add the lemon/lime juice to the eggs. Whisk.

13. When the crust is done, carefully remove it from the oven.

14. Pour the lemon/lime mixture over the crust.

15. Return the pan to the oven and bake for an additional 20-25 minutes, until the mixture no longer jiggles.

16. Remove from the oven and allow to cool completely.

17. Place the ½ cup of confectioner's sugar into a sifter or small sieve. Shake it over the lemon lime bars to give them a thick and even coating of sugar. Cut into squares.

Makes: 24 lemon lime bars

Peanut Butter Cookies

Dairy or Parve

Equipment list:

- 2 cookie sheets
- parchment paper
- measuring cups and spoons
- medium mixing bowl
- whisk
- large mixing bowl
- electric mixer
- wooden spoon or silicone spatula
- fork
- small glass

Ingredient list:

- 1¼ cups all-purpose flour
- ½ teaspoon baking soda
- ½ teaspoon baking powder
- ¼ teaspoon salt
- 8 tablespoons (1 stick) butter or margarine, softened
- ½ cup sugar
- ½ cup dark brown sugar
- 1 large egg
- ½ cup creamy peanut butter
- 1 teaspoon pure vanilla extract

These cookie are packed with peanut butter flavor and won't last very long. For a variation when you make them dairy, bake for 9 minutes, carefully remove the tray from the oven and press a chocolate chunk into the center of each cookie. Return the tray to the oven and bake for 1 final minute. You will definitely want a glass of cold milk to go with it.

1. Preheat the oven to 375° F.

2. Line the cookie sheets with parchment paper. Set aside.

3. Measure the flour, baking soda, baking powder, and salt into a medium mixing bowl.

4. With a whisk, mix the ingredients well and set them aside.

5. Place the butter or margarine into the bowl of a mixer or into a large mixing bowl.

6. Add the sugar and brown sugar.

7. With the mixer set to medium speed, cream the ingredients until they are light and fluffy. Add the egg, peanut butter, and vanilla. Mix again until very smooth, about 2 minutes, scraping down the bowl after a minute.

8. With a wooden spoon or silicone spatula stir in the flour mixture a little at a time until it is just mixed in and you don't see any traces of the flour.

9. Form heaping tablespoon-sized balls.

10. Place the balls of dough onto the prepared cookie sheets.

11. Fill a small glass with water. Dip a fork into the water. Gently press the fork down into each ball twice to make a criss-cross pattern and to flatten the cookies.

12. Place the cookie sheets into the oven and bake for 10-12 minutes.

13. Carefully remove the cookie sheets from the oven and allow the cookies to cool.

Makes: 25-30 cookies

Fruit Pockets

Parve

Equipment list:

- cookie sheet
- parchment paper
- measuring cups and spoons
- large mixing bowl
- whisk
- knife
- rolling pin
- 4-inch cookie cutter
- can opener
- fork
- sifter
- small mixing bowl

Ingredient list:

- 1 cup all-purpose flour
- ½ teaspoon salt
- ½ cup pure vegetable shortening, like Crisco®
- ¼ cup very cold water
- 1 small can cherry pie filling or apple pie filling
- ½ cup confectioner's sugar
- 3-4 teaspoons hot water

These little fruit pies taste fabulous. Once you get the hang of them, try using blueberry or strawberry pie filling or even experiment with fresh fruit. If you don't have a 4-inch round cookie cutter, measure the diameter of a large glass or ramekin. You can use those in place of the cookie cutter.

1. Preheat the oven to 350° F.

2. Line the cookie sheet with parchment paper. Set aside.

3. Place the flour and salt into a large mixing bowl. Mix with a whisk.

4. With a knife, cut the shortening into 8 pieces. Add the pieces of shortening to the bowl and with your fingertips, pinch the mixture until it becomes big crumbs of dough.

5. Add the cold water and knead with your hands until it becomes a smooth dough. Roll it into a ball. Try not to overwork the dough.

6. Place the dough on a sheet of parchment paper. Cover it with another sheet of parchment paper and press down. With a rolling pin, roll the dough between the two sheets. Get it nice and thin.

7. Remove the top sheet of parchment paper. With your cookie cutter or glass, cut out 4 circles. Re-roll the scraps of dough and cut out 4 more circles. Move 4 of the dough circles to the prepared cookie sheet.

8. With your can opener, open the can of pie filling. Place 1 tablespoon of pie filling in the center of

the 4 circles that are on the cookie sheet. Try to scoop out only the fruit, not the liquid. Pick up another circle of dough. Gently stretch it a little bit and place it over the top of one of the pie fillings. Repeat this with the other three.

9. With your fingers, go around the edges of each fruit pocket and press the dough together so that the two pieces of dough stick together, enclosing the filling. Make sure it is tight or the liquid will leak out when you bake them.

10. With the tines of a fork, go around the edges again pressing down to reinforce the seal and to make pretty indentation marks in the dough.

11. Place into the hot oven and bake for 35 minutes.

12. When the fruit pockets are done, remove them from the oven and let them cool.

13. When the pockets are cool, prepare the glaze. Place a sifter over a small mixing bowl. Pour the confectioner's sugar through the sifter into the bowl. Add the water and stir with a fork or spoon. It will be hard to mix at first but then it will become a smooth glaze. With a quick flicking motion, drizzle this glaze over the fruit pockets with your fork. Allow to set.

Makes: 4 fruit pockets

Creamy Rice Pudding

Dairy

Equipment list:

- measuring cups and spoons
- medium pot with lid
- wooden spoon
- small mixing bowl
- whisk
- plastic wrap

Ingredient list:

- 5 cups whole or 2% milk
- ½ cup long-grain white rice (not instant or quick cooking rice)
- ½ cup sugar
- ¼ teaspoon salt
- 1 large egg
- ½ teaspoon pure vanilla extract
- ½ cup heavy cream
- cinnamon

Rice pudding is very easy to make; it just takes patience and a lot of stirring, but you will be rewarded with a pot of creamy deliciousness. You can serve it in pretty glasses to really impress your family.

1. Pour the milk into a medium pot. Add the rice, sugar, and salt.

2. Turn the heat to medium and bring the mixture to a boil. Watch it very carefully to make sure it does not boil over the top of the pot. If you see it rising, lift up the pot from the handle and turn the heat down.

3. Once the mixture boils, cover the pot, reduce the heat to low and simmer. Lift the lid to stir the mixture with a wooden spoon every few minutes for 50 minutes. Make sure you keep checking that it is not boiling over.

4. Turn the heat off.

5. Crack the egg into a small mixing bowl. Whisk in the vanilla and heavy cream.

6. Add ½ cup of the rice mixture into the egg mixture. Mix it well and then add this mixture back into the pot. Turn the heat back to low and cook covered, for 10 minutes mixing often, until the mixture is bubbling.

7. Remove from heat and scoop into individual glasses or a serving bowl.

8. Sprinkle the top with cinnamon. Cover with plastic wrap, letting the wrap touch the surface of the pudding. Chill in the refrigerator.

Makes: 6 servings

Index